Dress Your Gingerbread

Bake Them!   Dress Them!   Eat Them!

Dress Your Gingerbread

Bake Them!   Dress Them!   Eat Them!

Joanna Farrow

spruce

An Hachette UK Company
First published in Great Britain in 2010 by Spruce
a division of Octopus Publishing Group Ltd
Endeavour House, 189 Shaftesbury Avenue,
London, WC2H 8JY

www.octopusbooks.co.uk

Distributed in the U.S.A. and Canada for Octopus
Books USA
c/- Hachette Book Group USA
237 Park Avenue
New York, NY 10017

Publisher: Sarah Ford
Managing Editor: Camilla Davis
Cover design and book development: Eoghan O'Brien
Designer: Michelle Tilly
Photography: Lis Parsons
Food Styling: Joanna Farrow
Production: Caroline Alberti

ISBN 13 978-1-84601-369-0
ISBN 10 1-84601-369-0

Printed and bound in China

10 9 8 7 6 5 4 3 2 1

This book includes dishes made with nuts and nut
derivatives. It is advisable for those with known allergic
reactions to nuts and nut derivatives and those who
may be potentially vulnerable to these allergies, such
as pregnant and nursing mothers, invalids, the elderly,
babies, and children, to avoid dishes made with nuts
and nut oils. It is also prudent to check the labels of
prepared ingredients for the possible inclusion of nut
derivatives. Some icings include raw eggs. It is prudent
for the potentially vulnerable (as before) to avoid raw
or lightly cooked eggs. Small candies are suggested as
decoration. Care should be taken if used by or served to
small children.

Conversion table and glossary

US and UK measures differ, so we have provided
here a summary of conversions you may require
when baking gingerbread or making the icings.

Ingredients

- $^3/_4$ cup all-purpose flour = 100 g
- $^1/_3$ cup confectioners' sugar = 50 g
- $1^1/_2$ cups confectioners' sugar = 200 g
- $4^1/_4$ cups confectioners' sugar = 500 g

Oven temperature

- 350°F / 180°C / Gas 4

Lengths

- $^1/_2$ inch = 1 cm
- 1 inch = 2.5 cm
- 2 inches = 5 cm
- 5 inches = 12.5 cm

Glossary

- Confectioners' sugar = icing sugar
- Corn syrup = golden syrup
- All-purpose flour = plain flour
- Hard candies = boiled sweets
- Semisweet chocolate = plain chocolate
- Dragees = sugar balls
- Glucose syrup = liquid glucose

Contents

Baking Gingerbread

F ew of us ever grow out of the enjoyment and childlike satisfaction we get from decorating cookies. Gingerbread men, with their classic chubby forms, are perfect for "dressing up" in almost any fun design. All you need to do is bake a batch of basic gingerbreads, gather an assortment of candy icings and decorations, and start assembling your own characters. There's certainly no better way to spend a bit of quality time, particularly if you have a "little one" to share the pleasure with. Creative skills are not obligatory, so you can follow the recipes accurately or use them as an inspirational starting point for your own. The cookies, once "dressed up," look colorful and special, some even slightly amusing! All serve numerous purposes once the decorating fun is over, whether they are enjoyed as a teatime treat, boxed up prettily for edible gifts, or used as a centerpiece for a special occasion.

TIP:

Stored in an airtight container the cookies will stay crisp for a couple of days. If they do start to soften, pop them onto a baking sheet and place in a moderate oven for a few minutes to re-crisp.

Ingredients

- 3 tablespoons softened unsalted butter
- 3 tablespoons light brown sugar
- 1 egg yolk
- 2 tablespoons corn syrup
- ¾ cup all-purpose flour
- ½ –1 teaspoon ground ginger

The recipe

This dough recipe makes enough for 4 gingerbread cookies, though it can easily be doubled up to make a larger batch. Add the amount of ginger you prefer—for younger children you might want to leave it out altogether.

1.

Cream together the butter and sugar in a mixing bowl until smooth. Stir in the egg yolk and syrup. Tip in the flour and ginger and mix to a firm dough. (Alternatively, blend the butter and sugar together in a food processor, add the remaining ingredients, and blend until combined). Turn out onto a lightly floured surface and knead into a smooth dough.

2.

Wrap in plastic wrap and chill for 30 minutes. Grease a large baking sheet.

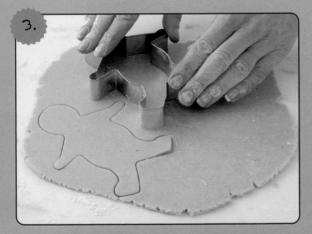

3.

Roll out the dough on a floured surface to about ¼-inch thickness. Cut out gingerbread shapes using a gingerbread cutter and space them slightly apart on the baking sheet. Reroll the trimmings to make more shapes.

4.

Bake in a preheated oven at 350°F for about 12–15 minutes until slightly darker in color and beginning to brown around the edges. Leave on the baking sheet for 5 minutes, then transfer to a cooling rack to cool.

Making Buttercream and Other Icings

All the icings used in the book are readily available in stores and online but are also easy to make at home.

Vanilla buttercream

This is used for spreading over gingerbread before covering with icing, as well as for piping decorations. It's easy to add food coloring to, and any leftover mixture will keep well in the refrigerator for a few days.

Ingredients

- 2 tablespoons unsalted butter, softened
- $1/3$ cup confectioners' sugar
- $1/4$ teaspoon vanilla extract
- 1 teaspoon boiling water

1. Beat the butter in a small bowl until smooth. Add the confectioners' sugar and vanilla, and beat until smooth.

2. Add the water and beat again until the texture is smooth and creamy, and paler in color.

Glacé icing

This is used for spreading over cookies before covering with fondant, and also for securing icings and other decorations in place. It can be used for piping but doesn't hold its shape as well as royal icing.

Ingredients

- $1/3$ cup confectioners' sugar
- 2 teaspoons lemon juice or cold water

1. Put the confectioners' sugar in a bowl. (If it has settled in the box and is a little lumpy, it can be sifted first.)

2. Add the lemon juice or water a little at a time until the consistency is smooth and the icing just holds its shape.

Ingredients

- 1 medium egg white
- 1½ cups confectioners' sugar

Royal icing

Royal icing sugar mix is available in some supermarkets and in specialty cake decorating stores. Follow package directions for the amount of water to add to make the icing. Royal icing can be stored in the refrigerator for several days and is ideal for piping decorations. You can also use it instead of bought decorator frosting tubes, with the advantage that you can make up any color. Simply add the required shade of food coloring and put in a paper pastry bag (see page 13). Royal icing is also used for "flooding" areas with icing. This technique requires a softer consistency (see page 16).

I. Put the egg white in a bowl and beat lightly to break it up. Add half the confectioners' sugar and beat until smooth.

2. Gradually work in the remaining confectioners' sugar until the icing has a thick, smooth consistency that just holds its shape.

Ingredients

- 1 medium egg white
- 2 tablespoons glucose syrup or light corn syrup
- About 4¼ cups confectioners' sugar

Homemade rolled fondant

This icing is used frequently in the book as it's so easy to make, color, and use (see page 10). If you prefer ready-to-use rolled fondant, it can be found in local stores or purchased through online bakery and craft suppliers.

I. Put the egg white, glucose or light corn syrup, and about a quarter of the confectioners' sugar in a bowl and mix to a smooth paste.

2. Continue to mix in more confectioners' sugar until it becomes too stiff to stir. Turn the paste out onto the work surface and knead in more confectioners' sugar to make a smooth, stiff paste. (If too soft and sticky the icing will be difficult to work with.)

3. Wrap tightly in several thicknesses of plastic wrap, unless you're going to be using it immediately.

Decorating Techniques

The following pages explain in more detail the techniques that are used frequently in the recipes. All are easy to master, even for first-time decorators.

Melting chocolate

Melted chocolate can be spread onto gingerbread with a spatula for a simple decoration and is also used for piping.

To melt chocolate in a pastry bag: If you've filled a bag with melted chocolate and it's started to set before you've used it all, the bag can be microwaved briefly to soften the chocolate. Don't do this, though, if the bag is fitted with a metal tip.

To melt in a microwave: Break the chocolate into chunks and put in a microwave-proof bowl. Melt in 1 minute spurts, checking frequently, until the chocolate is partially melted. Remove from the microwave and stir frequently until all the chocolate is melted. Take care when melting white chocolate, because it is more likely to burn due to the high sugar content.

To melt on the stove: Chop the chocolate into small pieces and put in a heatproof bowl. Set the bowl over a saucepan of gently simmering water, making sure the base of the bowl doesn't come in contact with the water. Once the chocolate starts to melt, turn off the heat and leave until completely melted, stirring from time to time until no lumps remain.

Using rolled fondant

Great fun to use, this icing is soft and pliable. It can be molded, or rolled out and cut into any shapes. Use a little confectioners' sugar to dust the work surface before you start, or your fingers if molding shapes. This will stop the icing sticking to the surface or your hands, particularly on a warm day. Any icing that's not being worked with should be wrapped in plastic wrap as it quickly dries out and its texture will be spoilt. If it does dry out on the surface because it hasn't been completely sealed, cut off and discard the edges, and the center should still be soft and pliable.

Adding color

Rolled fondant is readily available in white and basic colors, or in a wider range of colors from specialty cake decorating stores or online suppliers. In many of the gingerbread recipes you only need a small amount of certain colors so it makes better sense to color your own. Liquid food colors are generally acceptable for adding a pastel shade, but for stronger colors, paste food colors are more effective.

Dot the color onto the icing with a toothpick and knead it in on a surface dusted with confectioners' sugar. Use the color sparingly at first until you're sure of the strength of the food coloring—you can always blend in more if you want a more vibrant shade. If not using immediately, wrap tightly in plastic wrap.

Blending colors

Basic primary colors can be kneaded together to create more unusual colors. Use the same principle as mixing paints. Red and yellow can be mixed to make orange, blue and red to make purple, red and white to make pink, and black and white to make gray.

Finishing Touches

A few of the recipes use silver or gold food coloring. These are available as liquids, which require a good stir before use, or as powders, which should be mixed with a drop of vegetable oil to give a paint-like texture. Colored "dusting powders," such as the pink one used on the Princess's dress, add a shimmering texture (see page 48). The confectioner's glaze used on the Rock Star's leather pants, gives a shiny finish that loses its sticky texture once dry (see page 110). All these finishes are optional but worth buying for a special occasion.

Tube frostings

Tubes of decorator frosting feature widely in this book. Available in various colors and in chocolate flavors, they're so easy and convenient for piping directly onto the gingerbread. Simply squeeze the frosting to the nozzle end of the tube before you start so the frosting flows out in a steady line.

Piping frostings

Color the icing if required and spoon into a pastry bag, either reusable or paper. The reusable ones must be fitted with a writing or star pastry tip before use. Paper pastry bags (see opposite) are easy to use and only require a tip if piping star shapes. For writing purposes, simply snip off the tip of the bag. Take care not to snip off too much or the icing will flow out in too thick a line.

Making a paper pastry bag

Icings such as royal icing and buttercream are great for piping. Use a reusable pastry bag or make your own paper version out of parchment or wax paper.

Cut out a 10-inch square of parchment or wax paper. Fold it diagonally in half and then cut the paper in half along the fold. Take one triangle and hold it with the long edge facing away from you and holding the point nearest you with one hand.

Curl the right-hand point over to meet the center point, shaping a cone.

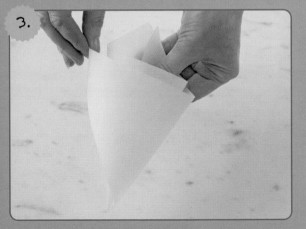

Bring the left-hand point over the cone so the three points meet.

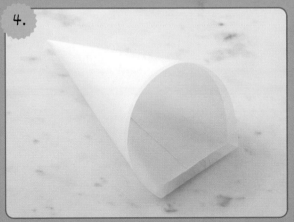

Fold the points over several times so the cone shape is secured in place.

Filling and using a paper pastry bag

If using a pastry tip, cut off about $^3/_4$ inch from the point of the bag and insert the pastry tip. Half fill the pastry bag with icing and twist the open end together to secure. If using for writing, snip off the merest tip so the icing flows out in a thin line. (This is particularly important if piping hair or fine details.) Hold the bag so that you keep the twisted end firmly closed and pipe as required.

Spreading buttercream

A small, flexible spatula is perfect for spreading buttercream. Be aware of the finished design before you start smoothing it over the different parts of the cookies, as you don't want it to show on areas that won't be iced.

Rolling and cutting rolled fondant

The trimmings after you've cut out your gingerbread can be rerolled, but wrap in plastic wrap so it doesn't dry out.

Lightly dust the work surface with confectioners' sugar and thinly roll out the required amount of icing. Ideally the fondant should be no more than about $^1/_{16}$ inch thick.

Shapes can either be cut out with a knife or, for larger areas, with the gingerbread cookie cutter. First rub the edges of the gingerbread cutter lightly with confectioners' sugar so it doesn't stick to the fondant.

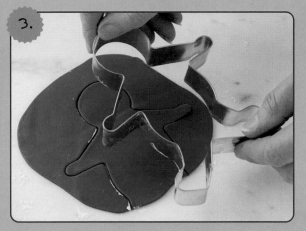

For cookies that require a jacket or pants shape to be cut, such as the Soccer Star or Firefighter (see pages 92 and 104), hover the cutter over the biscuit before pressing down so you're only cutting out the required area.

Once the cutter is lifted away, trim the fondant as required—at the waist, ankles, wrists, and neckline. Cookies will have expanded slightly during baking, so you might want to then roll the fondant a little thinner to cover the whole area.

Cutting out small decorations

Most of the small decorations are cut out with a knife. If using a cutter, such as a round one for shaping a skirt, dip the cutter in confectioners' sugar first so it doesn't stick to the fondant. For shapes like shoes or boots, it's easiest to use the gingerbread cutter as a guide, trimming off the excess.

Shaping frills

To create a delicate "frilly" edge, dust a wooden toothpick lightly with confectioners' sugar and run it horizontally along the edge of the fondant so that it starts to ruffle. Lift the fondant from the surface and redust so the ruffle doesn't stick, then roll with the toothpick again. Repeat until you have your preferred amount of frills. Trim off the unruffled edge if it becomes uneven. Once positioned, the ruffles can be lifted and folded with the tip of a toothpick.

Securing shapes in place

Where rolled fondant is laid onto a cookie, the surface should first be spread with a little glacé icing or buttercream (see page 8) to serve as a "glue." Don't spread the icing too thickly or the fondant won't be as easy to arrange in place. Where fondant is secured to another layer of icing, it's best to very lightly brush the fondant with a paintbrush, which you have dampened by dipping in a dish of cold water and brushed against the side of the dish to remove the excess. If too much water is left on the brush the icing won't stay neatly in place and the texture of the icing will be spoiled.

Flooding shapes with royal icing

Some of the clothing is made by "flooding" an outline of royal icing with a slightly thinner consistency of royal icing (see page 9).

1. 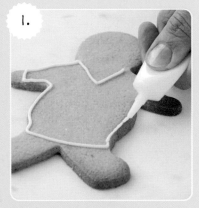	**2.** 	**3.** 
Once you've piped the outline (either using a tube of decorator frosting or piped royal icing), put a little more royal icing in a small bowl, adding color if the recipe requires.	Add a few drops of cold water so that the icing becomes smooth and level after a few seconds once you've stopped stirring it. Take care not to add too much water as the icing will quickly become too thin to manage.	Put the thinned icing in a paper pastry bag and snip off a small tip. Pipe into the area, spreading the icing into the corners with a toothpick. For a perfect finish, ideally the icing should be left to set for a few hours.

Making and using templates

Where it is helpful, template shapes are included either with the instructions for decorating the cookies or on pages 126–7. Trace the shape onto parchment paper and cut out—wax paper and tracing paper can also be used. Gently rest the shape over a little thinly rolled fondant (or candy or chocolate in some of the designs) and carefully cut around using a small sharp knife. Secure the shape in place.

Leaving shapes to harden

Rolled fondant decorations that extend beyond the edges of the gingerbread cookies can be left to harden for several hours on a sheet of parchment paper—it depends on how keen you are to create perfect results. If you're simply having a little fun decorating cookies, and they don't need to be perfect, you might want to secure them in place straight away, but for a special occasion you might prefer to let them harden first.

Choosing candy decorations

Many of the gingerbread designs include small candies for adding finishing touches. Generally, the smaller the candies, the more effective they are for adding touches like buckles, buttons, eyes, and jewelry. Most of the candies, particularly soft chews and gummy candies, can be cut into small pieces so their size works better with the proportions of the gingerbread cookie. Thin chewy candies can also be cut with scissors for shaping decorations like the Chef's hat and Nurse's apron (see pages 106 and 90).

Useful Equipment

Making and decorating gingerbread requires minimal equipment. Here are a few useful items that you might have already or want to buy.

Gingerbread cutters

The recipes are all designed for decorating a classic gingerbread man shape, about 5 inches in height. Bear in mind that both cookie and decorating quantities will be different if you use smaller or larger cutters.

Decorating cutters

Some of the recipes require small round cutters for cutting rolled fondant. These are available in various sizes (as small as $1/4$ inch) and give a neat, clean-edged circle.

Rolling pin

A regular pastry rolling pin is fine for rolling out the gingerbread dough, but for rolling small pieces of fondant a smaller rolling pin is easier to manage. Those included in kids' baking kits are ideal, or use a cake decorator's rolling pin, available from specialty stores.

Ruler

A metal or plastic ruler is useful for measuring lengths accurately, preventing guesswork!

Paintbrushes

Fine-tipped paintbrushes are ideal for painting food coloring onto icing. They're also used in many of the recipes that use rolled fondant, for securing decorations in place.

Parchment paper

This is used for making pastry bags (see page 13), for tracing templates, and as a surface for icing shapes to harden on, as the paper doesn't stick to the icing.

Spatula

A small flexible spatula is useful for spreading icing or chocolate over a cookie when you want a fairly smooth surface for adding more decorations. It's also useful for adding texture such as animal fur.

Icing pens

These resemble felt tip pens but are filled with edible food coloring and are useful for piping details onto icing. They can be used while the icing is still soft, but it is easier to pipe onto icing that has hardened.

Toothpicks

These are useful for dotting paste food coloring onto rolled fondant before kneading in. They're also used for easing royal icing into corners when spreading the icing over cookies and shaping frills (see page 15). Small metal skewers can be used instead.

Pastry bags

The recipes in this book are designed for using small paper pastry bags. These are disposable, require no tips for piping lines, and are easy to make (see Making a paper pastry bag, page 13). They can also be bought from cookware and cake decorating stores. If you prefer, use washable bags, which are reusable but must be fitted with either a writing or star tip before use.

Freezer bags

A small plastic freezer food bag makes a useful, shortcut improvisation for a pastry bag. Spoon the icing into one corner of the freezer bag and twist the bag so the icing is pushed right into the corner with no air spaces. Cut off the merest tip for piping.

Pastry tips

These enable you to pipe different shapes onto cookies. They're available in many different designs, although the only ones required for this book are a "star" tip, which can be used to pipe small star shapes or ridged lines, or a "writing" tip for piping straight or curvy lines, small buttons, hair, or other more detailed decorations.

Small sharp knife

A small cook's knife is useful for cutting out little fondant shapes and for cutting candies into smaller pieces. The sharp, fine-edged tip of a craft knife can be used instead for cutting out small, intricate shapes from rolled fondant where a larger knife might be less precise. Always work on a chopping board when using, as the sharp point can easily damage a work surface.

Teddy Bear

Ingredients

- 3 oz milk chocolate, melted (see page 10)
- 4 gingerbread cookies
- 4 milk chocolate disks, halved
- Chocolate-flavor sprinkles
- 2 oz white chocolate, melted (see page 10)
- 4 small round chocolate-flavor candies, halved
- 8 mini chocolate chips
- Tubes of black and red decorator frosting

Equipment

- Small spatula

Fur and ears: Using a spatula, spread a little milk chocolate across the tops of the gingerbread heads. While still soft, secure half a chocolate disk for each ear. Spread the rest of each gingerbread cookie with melted milk chocolate, avoiding the tummy, snout, and paw areas. While the chocolate is still soft, sprinkle it with plenty of chocolate-flavor sprinkles, pressing them down gently onto the chocolate.

Tummy, snout, and paws: Using a spatula, spread a little melted white chocolate over the tummy and snout areas, spreading it to fill out the shape. Spread a little more over all the paws.

Face: Thinly slice small round candies for eyes and secure in place using leftover melted chocolate. Add mini chocolate chips for the centers of the eyes. Pipe noses and mouths using black decorator frosting. Pipe little red tongues in red decorator frosting.

Bow tie: Use red decorator frosting to pipe the outlines of bow ties, then fill in the centers with more piping.

Sounds delicious!

Snazzy bow tie!

Grrrrrrowly tummy!

Guess who's coming to play...

Rag Doll

Ingredients

- Blue food coloring
- Double quantity vanilla buttercream (see page 8)
- 4 gingerbread cookies
- Tube of red decorator frosting
- 2 oz white chocolate, melted (see page 10)
- 2 oz milk chocolate, melted (see page 10)
- 8 mini chocolate chips

Equipment

- 3 paper pastry bags (see page 13)
- Small spatula

Dress: Beat blue food coloring into the buttercream, adding a little at a time until the desired shade is reached. Put half in a paper pastry bag and snip off the merest tip. Use to pipe the outline of a pinafore onto each gingerbread cookie. Pipe more buttercream to fill the bodice areas and then, using a spatula, spread the remaining blue buttercream to fill the skirt areas.

Stockings and shoes: Pipe horizontal lines of red decorator frosting across the legs, leaving a small gap between each line. Put a little melted white chocolate in a paper pastry bag and snip off the merest tip. Pipe lines of white chocolate between the lines of red frosting.

Put a little melted milk chocolate in a third paper pastry bag and snip off the merest tip. Use to pipe shoes at the bottom of each foot, adding little buttons in red decorator frosting.

Blouse: Use more white chocolate in the pastry bag to pipe the outline of a frilly blouse beneath the pinafore. Pipe the red detail on the cuffs with red decorator frosting.

Hair: Use the remaining milk chocolate to pipe bangs (a fringe) across the top of the heads and then two long thick braids. Finish the braids with red bows at the ends using the red decorator frosting.

Hat: Pipe a mop cap over the top of the heads using white chocolate. Finish the hat with a band of red decorator frosting across it.

Face: Make eyes with blobs of melted white chocolate, adding mini chocolate chips for the centers. Use red decorator frosting to pipe the mouths, noses, and red cheeks.

Cow

Ingredients

- Vanilla buttercream (see page 8)
- 4 gingerbread cookies
- Black food coloring
- 2 oz brown rolled fondant
- Confectioners' sugar, for dusting
- Small piece of orange rolled fondant
- Small piece of blue rolled fondant

Equipment

- Small spatula
- Paper pastry bag (see page 13)
- Craft knife

Body: Using a spatula, spread a thin layer of buttercream over each gingerbread cookie, leaving the sides of the heads uncovered. Beat black food coloring into the remaining buttercream, adding a little at a time until the desired shade is reached. Put some in a paper pastry bag and snip off the merest tip. Use to pipe irregular outlines of black markings over the body areas. Fill in the shapes with more buttercream.

Face: Shape 4 grape-size pieces of brown fondant into oval shapes and press onto the lower halves of the faces. Impress small mouths with the tip of a craft knife and pipe small black nostrils. Shape and position small ears in brown fondant. Pipe eyes in black buttercream and press tiny balls of blue fondant into the centers. Use more black buttercream to pipe the centers of the eyes.

Horns: For each set of horns, roll a little orange fondant under your fingertips until $1^3/_4$ inches long, tapering to a point at the ends. Bend the ends over and position at the top of each head.

Hooves: Use more black buttercream to pipe the outlines of hooves, then fill them in with more buttercream.

try me too! page 84

Great for
grazing!

Udderly scrumptious!

Sheep

Ingredients

- 2 oz yellow rolled fondant
- 4 gingerbread cookies
- Vanilla buttercream
  (see page 8)
- 8 small hard candies
- 1 oz brown rolled fondant
- Confectioners' sugar, for
  dusting
- Black food coloring

Equipment

- Craft knife
- 2 paper pastry bags
  (see page 13)

Face: Shape 4 cherry-size pieces of yellow fondant into oval shapes and secure to the head of each gingerbread cookie with a little buttercream. Shape 8 tiny ovals of yellow fondant and pinch together at one end. Use a little buttercream to secure in place for ears. Impress small mouths into the yellow fondant with the tip of a craft knife.

Press 2 small hard candies into the fondant for eyes. Roll tiny balls of the brown fondant and press onto the eyes. Put 2 tablespoons of the buttercream in a bowl and beat in some black food coloring, adding a little at a time until the desired shade is reached. Put in a paper pastry bag and snip off the merest tip. Use to pipe nostrils and the centers of the eyes.

Hooves and legs: Shape 4 hooves for each cookie by rolling a pea-size piece of brown fondant on a surface dusted with confectioners' sugar and cutting a notch out of one side. Secure in place with a little buttercream from the piping bag. Cut a little extra off the piping bag so the buttercream flows in a thicker line and use to pipe thin legs extending from the hooves, each about $^3/_4$ inch long.

Body: Put the rest of the buttercream in a paper pastry bag and snip off the merest tip. Use to cover the body with plenty of curly lines of piping, adding a few more curls to the tops of the heads.

Ladybug

Ingredients

- 3 oz black rolled fondant
- Confectioners' sugar, for dusting
- 4 gingerbread cookies
- Vanilla buttercream (see page 8)
- Small piece of white rolled fondant
- 8 small jelly beans
- 4 oz red rolled fondant
- 5 oz green rolled fondant (optional)

Equipment

- Parchment paper, for tracing
- Pencil
- Scissors
- Rolling pin
- Craft knife
- Small spatula
- Paintbrush

Face: Trace and cut out the Ladybug's head template (see opposite). Roll out a little of the black fondant on a surface dusted with confectioners' sugar until about $1/16$ inch thick. Cut around the template, and repeat to give 4 heads. Secure the heads in place with buttercream.

Mold large round eyes in white fondant and secure in place with buttercream. Push a small jelly bean into the center of each. Add small red mouths, made from tiny pieces of red fondant.

Body: Roll out the remaining red fondant and cut out 4 egg shapes that are the same size as the gingerbread bodies. Using a spatula, spread buttercream over the body area of each gingerbread cookie and secure the fondant in place. Add a strip of black fondant down the center of each, securing with a dampened paintbrush. Flatten small balls of black icing for spots and secure in place with the dampened paintbrush.

Legs: Secure 4 thin strips of black fondant extending from the body of each ladybug, as in the picture. Take 8 cherry-size balls of black fondant and flatten into oval shapes for the feet. Secure in place with buttercream.

Leaf: If making leaves, thinly roll out the green fondant and cut out a leaf shape, cutting little notches around the edges. Use a craft knife to mark a line down the middle of the leaf. These are best left to harden on a sheet of parchment paper for several hours. Rest the ladybugs over the leaves.

Big bug eyes!

Spotty shell!

Don't forget to eat your greens!

Who's at the bottom of the garden?

Bumblebee

Ingredients

- 4 gingerbread cookies
- 4 oz chocolate-flavored or brown rolled fondant
- Confectioners' sugar, for dusting
- Vanilla buttercream (see page 8)
- Brown food coloring
- 3 oz yellow rolled fondant
- Small piece of white rolled fondant
- 4 sheets of rice paper

Equipment

- Toothpicks
- Parchment paper, for tracing
- Pencil
- Scissors
- Rolling pin
- Craft knife
- Paintbrush

Antenna: The antenna are best fixed when the gingerbread cookies come out of the oven and are still soft. For each set of antennae, break a toothpick in half. Gently press 2 into the top of each cookie, then allow to cool before decorating.

Trace and cut out the Bumblebee's head template (see opposite). Roll out a little of the chocolate-flavored or brown fondant on a surface dusted with confectioners' sugar until about $1/16$ inch thick. Cut around the template, and repeat to give 4 heads. Secure in place with buttercream.

Paint the toothpicks brown with food coloring. Roll 8 pea-size balls of brown fondant and push onto the ends of the toothpicks.

Body: Roll out the yellow fondant and cut out 4 egg shapes that are the same size as the gingerbread bodies. Secure in place with buttercream. Cut curved strips of the rolled out brown fondant and position over the yellow, securing with a dampened paintbrush. Trim off the excess.

Legs: Secure 2 thin strips of brown fondant extending from the body of each bumblebee. Take 8 cherry-size balls of brown fondant and flatten into oval shapes for the feet. Secure in place with buttercream.

Face: Mold 4 cherry-size balls of yellow fondant and flatten onto the lower half of each face, securing with a little buttercream. Shape the white fondant into eyes and mouths and secure in place with a dampened paintbrush. Paint the center of the eyes, nose, and mouth with brown food coloring.

Wings: Fold a sheet of rice paper in half and cut out wings. Open out and secure to the backs of the bumblebees with buttercream.

Tabby Cat

Ingredients

- 1 tablespoon cocoa powder
- Double quantity vanilla buttercream (see page 8)
- 4 gingerbread cookies
- 2 chocolate mints
- Black and orange food coloring

Equipment

- Small spatula
- Craft knife
- 3 paper pastry bags (see page 13)

Body: Beat the cocoa powder into two-thirds of the buttercream. Using a spatula, spread the chocolate-flavored buttercream over each gingerbread cookie, leaving the hands, feet, tummies, and centers of the faces uncovered. Spread a little vanilla buttercream over these uncoated areas and fluff up lightly with a spatula.

Face and ears: Using a craft knife, cut the corners off the chocolate mints and press into the buttercream for ears. Beat some black food coloring into a third of the remaining buttercream, adding a little at a time until the desired shade is reached. Put in a paper pastry bag and snip off the merest tip. Use to pipe eyes, snouts, and whiskers onto the faces.

Fur: Beat orange food coloring into half the remaining buttercream, adding a little at a time until the desired shade is reached. Put in a paper piping bag and snip off the merest tip. Put the remaining buttercream in a paper pastry bag and snip off the merest tip. Use the black, orange, and vanilla buttercreams to pipe wiggly lines outward from each cat's tummy.

try me too! page 56

Easter Bunny

Ingredients

- 4 tablespoons sugar
- Yellow food coloring
- 3 oz white chocolate, melted (see page 10)
- 4 gingerbread cookies
- 3 oz yellow marzipan
- 6 white mini marshmallows
- 1 tablespoon chocolate hazelnut spread
- 12 small round colored candies
- 16 small chocolate eggs

Equipment

- Small spatula
- 2 paper pastry bags (see page 13)
- Craft knife

Body: Put the sugar in a bowl and add a little yellow food coloring. Using the back of a teaspoon, work the color into the sugar until evenly blended. Using a spatula, spread a thin layer of melted white chocolate over each of the gingerbread cookies, leaving the hands uncovered. Sprinkle a generous layer of the sugar over the chocolate and press it down gently. Tip off any loose sugar.

Face: Take 4 cherry-size balls of marzipan and cut in half. Mold each into a long ear shape. Take another 4 cherry-size pieces of marzipan and flatten each into an oval shape, about $1^3/4$ inches long and $3/4$ inch wide. Squeeze together slightly in the center. Put a little more melted white chocolate in a paper pastry bag and snip off the merest tip. Pipe a little over each gingerbread head and position the marzipan pieces as in the picture. Pipe the centers of the ears with more chocolate.

Using a craft knife, cut 4 white mini marshmallows in half and secure in place with chocolate from the piping bag for eyes. Next, spoon a little chocolate hazelnut spread into a paper pastry bag, and snip off the tip. Use to pipe the centers of the eyes and some whiskers on the nose.

For the teeth, shape pieces of the remaining marshmallows into rectangles, as small as you can cut them. Secure in place with piped white chocolate.

Finishing touches: Pipe a band of white chocolate along each wrist and across the bottoms of the feet. Pipe 3 dots of chocolate down the front of each rabbit and position small candies for buttons. Rest 6 chocolate eggs around the arms and the head.

What's up choc?!

Hopping delicious!

Guess who's around the corner... 👉

Mrs Claus

Ingredients

- Tubes of green, red, and white decorator frosting
- 4 gingerbread cookies
- A little strawberry jelly
- 3 oz red rolled fondant
- Confectioners' sugar, for dusting
- Small piece of dark green rolled fondant
- Small piece of blue rolled fondant
- Edible silver or gold food coloring

Equipment

- Small spatula
- Rolling pin
- Craft knife
- Toothpick
- Paintbrush

Body: Use green decorator frosting to pipe the outline of a blouse, including a collar, onto each gingerbread cookie. Fill in the collars with white decorator frosting and pipe dots for buttons. Pipe dots of red decorator frosting over the blouses.

Apron: Using a spatula, spread a little strawberry jelly over the apron area of each cookie. Roll out the red fondant on a surface dusted with confectioners' sugar until about $1/16$ inch thick. Cut out 4 rectangles, each measuring about $1^1/4$ x $3/4$ inches. Secure in place for the tops of the aprons. Cut out 4 more rectangles of red fondant, each measuring about $2^1/2$ x 2 inches, and secure to the bottom halves of the cookies.

Make folds along the lower edges of the aprons by lifting the fondant at intervals with a toothpick and pinching the fondant around the toothpick so the folds are held in place.

Use thin strips of the red fondant trimmings to make straps over the shoulders and apron strings, finishing with a small bow to one side. Pipe green buttons at the top corners of the aprons and the outline of a pocket on each apron.

Slippers: Mold 8 little slippers out of dark green fondant and secure in place with dots of decorator frosting. Pipe "fluffy" edges to the slippers with white decorator frosting.

try me too! page 46

Hair: Use white decorator frosting to pipe hair, adding a "bun" shape to the top. Use red and green decorator frosting to pipe a holly decoration over the hair. Add more dots of red frosting for earrings.

Face: Pipe small blobs of white decorator frosting for the eyes. Mold tiny balls of blue fondant and secure them on top. Use red decorator frosting to pipe the noses and mouths, and white decorator frosting to pipe glasses. Once the frosting has hardened slightly, paint the glasses silver or gold with edible food coloring.

Santa Claus

Ingredients

- Red food coloring
- Double quantity vanilla buttercream (see page 8)
- 4 gingerbread cookies
- 1 licorice wheel
- 12 mini chocolate chips
- Tube of black decorator frosting
- 8 small blue candy drops

Equipment

- Small spatula
- Craft knife
- Paper piping bag (see page 13)
- Star tip

Suit: Beat the red food coloring into half the buttercream, adding a little at a time until the desired shade is reached. Using a spatula, spread a thin layer over each gingerbread cookie, leaving the head, hands, and feet uncovered.

Unroll the licorice wheel and cut 4 lengths to fit the width of the bodies for belts and press gently in place. Press 3 chocolate chips down the suit fronts for the buttons.

Put the remaining vanilla buttercream in a paper pastry bag fitted with a star tip, then pipe thick lines across the cuffs and lower edges of the red suits just above the legs.

Hat: Spread a little more red buttercream at a tilting angle across the top of each head. Pipe vanilla buttercream across two-thirds of the lower edges, as in the picture, and add a bobble at the other end.

Boots: Use black decorator frosting to pipe the outlines of the boots, then fill in with more piping. Next, pipe thick lines of vanilla buttercream across the top of the boots.

Face: Using the end of the spatula, dab a little red buttercream over the mouth area of the faces, then use more of the vanilla buttercream in the pastry bag to pipe mustaches and beards. Position the candies for eyes, securing in place with dots of the black decorator frosting, then pipe a dot of black decorator frosting into the center of each.

Buttercream beard!

Ho Ho Ho!
Merry munching!

Delicious chocolate drops

Season's eatings!

Turn over for more festive fun...

Snowman

Ingredients

- Royal icing (see page 9)
- 4 gingerbread cookies
- 4 chocolate mint sticks
- Tubes of black and green decorator frosting
- Small piece of gray rolled fondant
- Confectioners' sugar, for dusting
- Small piece of orange rolled fondant
- Small piece of red rolled fondant

Equipment

- Small spatula
- Parchment paper, for tracing
- Pencil
- Scissors
- Rolling pin
- Craft knife

Body: Using a spatula, spread a little royal icing over the legs of each gingerbread cookie, leaving the feet uncovered. Roll out the white fondant on a surface dusted with confectioners' sugar until about $1/16$ inch thick. Cut out 4 rectangles, each measuring about 3 x $1^1/4$ inches, and then secure across the legs covering the gap between them.

Spread more royal icing over the fondant rectangles, the bodies, and heads. Level and then texture it with the tip of the spatula.

Break the chocolate mint sticks into pieces to resemble twigs and arrange them over the arms, pushing them into the royal icing to hold them in place at the ends and adding dots of black decorator frosting under the chocolate to secure. Pipe dots of black decorator frosting down the fronts of the snowmen for buttons.

Hat: Trace and cut out the Snowman's hat template (see opposite). Roll out the gray fondant on a surface dusted with confectioner's sugar until about $1/16$ inch thick. Cut around the template. Repeat to give 4 hats. Secure at an angle on the heads and pipe a band of green decorator frosting across each hat.

Face: Mold 4 carrot-shaped noses in orange fondant, making shallow grooves around the sides with a craft knife to resemble carrots. Push into the faces. Pipe large blobs of black frosting for the eyes and rows of smaller dots for the mouths.

Scarf: Roll out the red fondant and cut into $3/4$-inch-wide strips. Cut into shorter lengths to make 4 scarves. Make fringes at the ends of each scarf by pressing the end of a toothpick into the fondant. Drape a scarf around each neck. Pipe lines of green decorator frosting across the scarves.

'Tis the season to be yummy!

Frosty frosting!

Reindeer

Ingredients

- 4 gingerbread cookies
- 1 oz chocolate-flavored or brown rolled fondant
- Confectioners' sugar, for dusting
- 3 oz milk chocolate, melted (see page 10)
- Small piece of light brown rolled fondant
- 3 oz semisweet chocolate, melted (see page 10)
- Small piece of black rolled fondant
- Small piece of red rolled fondant
- Silver dragees
- Tube of red decorator frosting
- Small piece of white rolled fondant
- Confectioner's glaze (optional)

Equipment

- Toothpicks
- Parchment paper, for tracing
- Pencil
- Scissors
- Rolling pin
- Craft knife
- Small spatula
- Paper pastry bag (see page 13)
- Paintbrush

Antlers: The antlers are best fixed when the gingerbread cookies come out of the oven and are still soft. For each set of antlers, break a toothpick in half. Gently press 2 into the top of each cookie. Allow to cool before decorating.

Trace and cut out the Reindeer antler templates (see opposite). Roll out the chocolate-flavored or brown fondant on a surface dusted with confectioners' sugar until about $^1/_{16}$ inch thick. Cut around the templates, and repeat to give 4 sets of antlers. Dampen the toothpicks with water and press the antlers onto them.

Body: Using a spatula, spread the milk chocolate all over each gingerbread body and the center of each head, leaving the arms and legs uncovered. Break off tiny pieces of the light brown fondant, roll into balls, and flatten slightly. Secure around the edges of the bodies, as in the picture.

Legs: Put the semisweet chocolate in a paper pastry bag and snip off the tip. Pipe thick lines of chocolate down each limb. For each hoof, take a pea-size ball of black fondant and flatten into a hoof shape. Make a cut into the base and secure at the end of the piped chocolate.

Collar: Roll out the red fondant and cut out 4 narrow strips, about $1^3/_4$ x $^1/_4$ inches. Secure around the necks of the reindeer and fix silver dragees on top using the red decorator frosting.

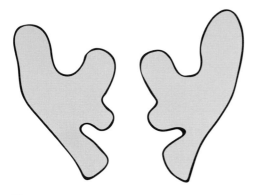

Face: For each snout, take a small piece of light brown fondant and shape into an oval, about $^3/_4$ inch long. Secure to the lower half of the face.

Roll small balls of white fondant for eyes. Flatten slightly and secure in place with decorator frosting. Roll thin lengths of black fondant under your fingertips and wrap around the eyes. Add more balls of black fondant for the centers of the eyes.

Position balls of red fondant for noses and pipe mouths underneath using the red decorator frosting. If desired, paint the noses with confectioner's glaze to make them shiny.

Angel

Wings and trumpets: Trace and cut out the Angel's wings and trumpet templates (see page 126 and opposite). Roll out the white fondant on a surface dusted with confectioners' sugar until about $\frac{1}{16}$ inch thick. Cut around the wings template, making 4 of each. From the trimmings, trace and cut out 4 trumpet shapes. Transfer all the shapes to a sheet of parchment paper to harden for several hours.

Dress: Using a spatula, spread a little buttercream over the body area of each gingerbread cookie. For each dress, thinly roll out a quarter of the pale blue fondant. Gently rest the gingerbread cutter over the surface of the fondant and use it as a guide to cutting out a dress shape. As you cut the shape out, include sleeve extensions and a curved edge around the neckline. Cut the fondant in a curved edge around the base. Secure in place.

Thinly roll out the white fondant trimmings and cut out tiny heart shapes with the cutter. Use to decorate the lower edge of the dresses, securing in place with a dampened paintbrush. Add a final heart at the neck of the dresses.

Hair and halo: Put the remaining buttercream in a paper pastry bag and snip off the merest tip. Use to pipe long wavy hair. Thinly roll out the pale blue fondant trimmings and cut into 4 very thin strips, about $2\frac{1}{2}$ inches long. Bend the ends into a halo shape and secure in place.

Face: Mold large eyes in white fondant to shape large eyes and secure in place with dots of buttercream. Roll tiny balls of blue fondant and press onto the eyes. Add small pink fondant noses and mouths.

Ingredients

- 3 oz white rolled fondant
- Confectioners' sugar, for dusting
- Vanilla buttercream (see page 8)
- 4 gingerbread cookies
- 5 oz pale blue rolled fondant
- Blue food coloring
- Small piece of pink rolled fondant
- Edible gold food coloring
- Edible pale blue dusting powder (optional)

Equipment

- Parchment paper, for tracing
- Pencil
- Scissors
- Rolling pin
- Craft knife
- Small spatula
- Gingerbread cutter
- Small heart-shaped cutter
- Paintbrush
- Paper pastry bag (see page 13)

Finishing touches: Secure the wings behind the angels with dots of buttercream. Secure the trumpets to the hands, then paint the trumpets and halos with gold food coloring. If using the dusting powder, lightly coat your fingertip with the powder, or use a paintbrush, and smooth it gently over the angels' dresses.

Elf

Ingredients

- Green and red food coloring
- Double quantity vanilla buttercream (see page 8)
- 4 gingerbread cookies
- 4 long thin chewy candies in pink, red, or green
- 4 small licorice candies
- 16 small round candies in red and green
- Tube of black decorator frosting
- 2 plain licorice candies

Equipment

- Small spatula
- Craft knife
- Paper pastry bag (see page 13)

Suit: Beat green food coloring into half the buttercream, adding a little at a time until the desired shade is reached. Beat red food coloring into the other half, again adding a little at a time until the desired shade is reached. Using a spatula, spread a thin layer of green buttercream over each gingerbread cookie, leaving the heads, hands, and feet uncovered.

Cut the chewy candies to the width of the bodies and press gently into position. Secure a licorice candy to the center of each with a dot of buttercream. Press 3 red or green candies down the suit fronts for buttons.

Put the red buttercream in a paper pastry bag and snip off the merest tip. Use to pipe the outlines of collars and cuffs onto the suits. Fill in the outlines with more piping.

Hat: Spread a little more green buttercream over the tops of the heads. Pipe an outline of red buttercream around the edges and secure another round candy to one side to make a bobble.

Face: Pipe more red buttercream to make the noses and mouths, and add dots of black decorator frosting for the eyes.

Boots: Use the red buttercream to pipe the outlines of boots, then fill in with more piping. Cut thin lengths of licorice candies and position across the tops of the boots.

Chewy candy Christmas hat!

Nice and naughty licorice!

Big buttercream boots!

Who else has been good this year?

Princess

Ingredients

- Small piece of dark pink rolled fondant
- Confectioners' sugar, for dusting
- 4 gingerbread cookies
- Vanilla buttercream (see page 8)
- Pink and silver dragees
- 5 oz pale pink rolled fondant
- Tube of white decorator frosting
- Edible pink dusting powder (optional)
- Small piece of white rolled fondant
- Small piece of blue rolled fondant

Equipment

- Rolling pin
- Small spatula
- Gingerbread cutter
- Craft knife
- Toothpick
- Paintbrush
- Paper pastry bag (see page 13)

Slippers: Roll out a little dark pink fondant on a surface dusted with confectioners' sugar until about $1/16$ inch thick. Cut out narrow slipper shapes. Secure to the gingerbread cookies with a little buttercream. Add a pink dragee to each slipper, securing with dots of white decorator frosting.

Dress: Using a spatula, spread a little buttercream over the body area of each cookie. For each dress, roll out a quarter of the pale pink fondant until about $1/16$ inch thick. Rest the cutter over the surface of the fondant and use it as a guide to cutting out a dress shape. As you cut the shape out, include sleeve extensions, a fluted edge around the neckline, and a curved edge around the base. Secure in place.

Make folds along the lower edges of the aprons by lifting the fondant at intervals with a toothpick and pinching the fondant around the toothpick so the folds are held in place.

Use white decorator frosting to pipe dots. Add pink dragees along the edges of the sleeves, securing with dots of decorator frosting. If using the dusting powder, lightly coat your fingertip with the powder and smooth it gently over the skirts.

Sash: Cut 4 long thin strips of dark pink fondant and secure around the waists with a dampened paintbrush.

Necklace: Use white decorator frosting to pipe necklaces, pressing a pink dragee into the center of each.

Hair: Put the remaining buttercream in a paper pastry bag and snip off the merest tip. Use to pipe hair, building it up in ringlets around each face.

Tiara: Press silver dragees gently into the hair while still soft.

Face: Shape tiny mouths in dark pink fondant, noses in pale pink fondant, and wide eyes using flattened balls of white and blue fondant. Secure with dots of decorator frosting. Pipe eyelashes using buttercream.

Monster

Ingredients

- Confectioners' sugar, for dusting
- 3 oz pale pink rolled fondant
- 4 gingerbread cookies
- Vanilla buttercream (see page 8)
- Green food coloring
- Small piece of brown or chocolate-flavored rolled fondant
- Small piece of white rolled fondant
- Brown food coloring
- Small piece of dark pink rolled fondant
- Tube of white decorator frosting

Equipment

- Small spatula
- Craft knife
- Paper pastry bag (see page 13)
- Toothpick
- Paintbrush

Tummy: Using hands dusted with confectioners' sugar, roll 4 balls of pale pink fondant, about the size of a whole walnut, and flatten into oval shapes. Using a spatula, spread buttercream over the tummy area of each gingerbread cookie and secure the fondant in place. Mark horizontal lines with the tip of a craft knife.

Fur: Beat green food coloring into the remaining buttercream, adding a little at a time until the desired shade is reached, and spread a little onto the faces. Put the remainder in a paper pastry bag and snip off the merest tip. Use to pipe squiggly lines around the edges of the face, tummy, and all over the rest of each cookie.

Horns and claws: Mold little pieces of chocolate-flavored or brown fondant into stumpy horns and claws, and press into the buttercream.

Face: Use flattened balls of white fondant for the eyes, painting the centers with brown food coloring. Use small balls of brown fondant for the noses, adding nostrils with the tip of a toothpick. Add a tiny piece of dark pink fondant for each mouth, outlining the edges with white decorator frosting.

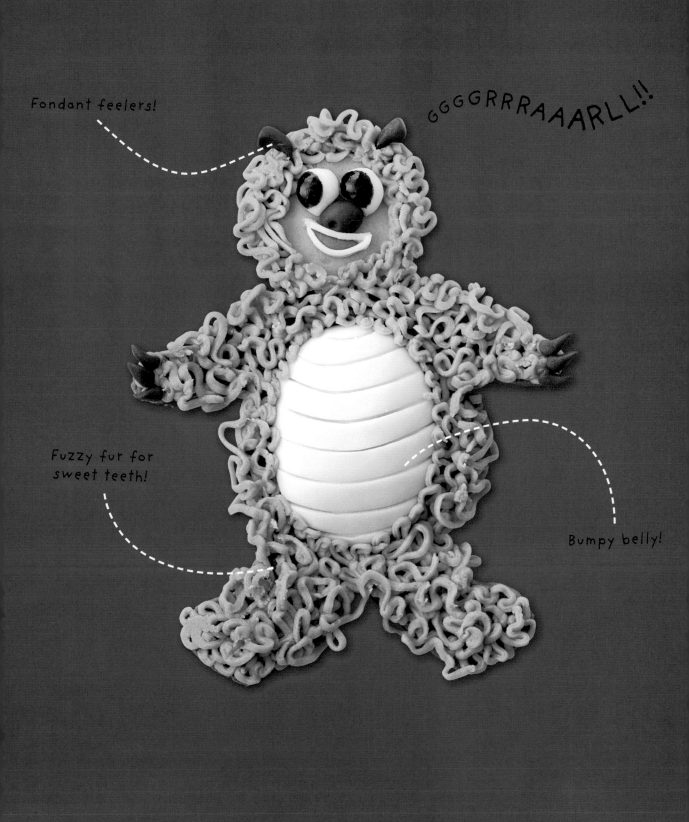

Fondant feelers!

GGGGRRRAAARLL!!

Fuzzy fur for sweet teeth!

Bumpy belly!

Mermaid

Ingredients

- 2 oz lilac rolled fondant
- Confectioners' sugar, for dusting
- 4 gingerbread cookies
- Vanilla buttercream (see page 8)
- Pink and blue dragees
- Tubes of white and yellow decorator frosting
- 4 oz turquoise rolled fondant
- 2 oz yellow rolled fondant
- Small piece of red rolled fondant
- Small piece of white rolled fondant
- Blue food coloring

Equipment

- Rolling pin
- Craft knife
- Parchment paper, for tracing
- Pencil
- Scissors
- Small spatula
- Small star cutter
- Paintbrush

Shell top: Roll out a little lilac fondant on a surface dusted with confectioners' sugar until about $\frac{1}{16}$ inch thick. Cut out 8 shell shapes, scoring the shell markings with the tip of a craft knife. Position 2 on each gingerbread cookie, securing in place with a little buttercream. Reroll the trimmings and add thin straps at the sides. Position a pink dragee in the center or the top, securing with a dot of white decorator frosting.

Tail: Trace and cut out the Mermaid's tail template (see page 126). Thinly roll out the turquoise fondant and cut around the template. Repeat to give 4 tails. Using a spatula, spread buttercream over the legs of each gingerbread cookie, and secure each tail in place. Pipe scale markings with yellow decorator frosting. Decorate the top edges with blue dragees, securing with dots of yellow decorator frosting.

Hair: Trace and cut out the Mermaid's hair template (see opposite). Thinly roll out the yellow fondant and cut around the template. Repeat to give 4 sets of hair. Secure in place with buttercream. Thinly roll out the red fondant and use a small star cutter to make the starfish hair decorations. Secure with yellow decorator frosting.

Face: Flatten 8 balls of white fondant for eyes, painting the centers with blue food coloring. Secure in place with dots of white decorating frosting, then pipe eyelashes with white decorating frosting. Shape tiny pieces of red fondant for mouths and secure with a dot of white decorator frosting.

Bracelet: Secure pink dragees to the wrists using dots of yellow decorator frosting.

Pretty pearl
bracelet!

Tails from
the deep!

Find out who's setting sail...

Pirate

Ingredients

- Vanilla buttercream (see page 8)
- 4 gingerbread cookies
- 2 oz white rolled fondant
- Confectioners' sugar, for dusting
- 4 oz red rolled fondant
- Small piece of lilac rolled fondant
- Tubes of black, white, and yellow decorator frosting
- Blue dragees
- 4 oz black rolled fondant
- Blue food coloring
- Small piece of turquoise rolled fondant

Equipment

- Small spatula
- Rolling pin
- Craft knife
- Paintbrush
- Gingerbread cutter
- Parchment paper, for tracing
- Pencil
- Scissors

T-shirt and belt: Using a spatula, spread a little buttercream over the top half of each gingerbread cookie, leaving the faces uncovered. Roll out the white fondant on a surface dusted with confectioners' sugar until about $1/16$ inch thick. Cut out 4 x $1^1/4$-inch squares. Secure in place for T-shirts.

Roll out a little red fondant and cut out thin strips. Lay them across the white fondant, securing with a dampened paintbrush. Secure a strip of lilac fondant under each T-shirt. Pipe a square of black decorator frosting on top and press blue dragees into the frosting for buckles.

Boots: For each pair of boots, thinly roll out a little of the black fondant. Press each leg of the gingerbread cutter into the fondant, trimming off the top edge in a straight line. Secure in place with buttercream. Add strips of black fondant around the legs at the top of the boots, securing with a dampened paintbrush.

Coat: For each coat, roll out a quarter of the remaining red fondant until about $1/16$ inch thick. Rest the gingerbread cutter over the surface of fondant and use it as a guide to cutting out a coat shape, trimming off the fondant at the neck and wrists, and cutting a straight line at the lower edge. Cut a $3/4$-inch-wide strip out of the front of each coat, then secured in place either side of the T-shirt with a dampened toothbrush.

Decorate the edges with thin strips of black fondant, securing with a dampened paintbrush. Add thick cuffs in black fondant and pipe buttons on the coat and cuffs in black decorator frosting.

Hat: Trace and cut out the Pirate's hat template (see opposite). Thinly roll out the remaining black fondant and cut around the template. Repeat to give 4 hats. Secure in place with buttercream, adding skull and crossbones designs with white decorator frosting.

Face: Shape and position eye patches, using the black fondant trimmings and securing with white decorator frosting. Add balls of white fondant for the eyes, painting the centers with blue food coloring. Position small black mouths with a few white fondant teeth, leaving gaps in between them.

Hair: Use yellow decorator frosting to pipe curly hair, mustaches, and beards.

Cutlass: Mold small handles for each cutlass in turquoise fondant and the blades in red. Secure to the hands with white decorator frosting.

Lion

Ingredients

- Vanilla buttercream (see page 8)
- 4 gingerbread cookies
- 5 oz yellow rolled fondant
- Confectioners' sugar, for dusting
- 3 oz chocolate-flavored or dark brown rolled fondant
- Small piece of light brown rolled fondant
- Small piece of white rolled fondant
- Orange food coloring
- Small piece of red rolled fondant
- Brown or black food coloring
- Small piece of purple rolled fondant
- Silver dragees

Equipment

- Small spatula
- Rolling pin
- Gingerbread cutter
- Craft knife
- Parchment paper, for tracing
- Pencil
- Scissors
- Paintbrush
- Paper pastry bag (see page 13)

Body: Using a spatula, spread the buttercream over the cookies. Roll out the yellow fondant on a surface dusted with confectioners' sugar until about $1/16$ inch thick. Cut out 4 gingerbread shapes with the cutter, trimming about $1/8$ inch from around the edge. Secure in place on each cookie.

Mane: Trace and cut out the Lion's mane template (see opposite). Thinly roll out the chocolate-flavored or dark brown fondant and cut around the template. Repeat to give 4 manes. Secure in place.

Face: Flatten pea-size rounds of light brown fondant. Trim slices off one side and position for ears. Do the same for the eyes, using white fondant. Add small, triangular-shaped noses in chocolate-flavored or dark brown fondant. Secure all pieces in place with a dampened paintbrush. Beat orange food coloring into the remaining buttercream, adding a little at a time until the desired shade is reached. Put in a paper pastry bag and snip off the merest tip. Use the orange buttercream to pipe the centers of the ears, mouths, and spots. Add small molded tongues in red fondant. Paint the eyes with dark brown or black food coloring.

Crown: Cut out 4 rectangles, about $3/4$ x $1/2$ inch, of purple fondant and cut deep triangles out of one edge. Secure in place with buttercream, opening out the points slightly. Secure a silver dragee to each point with a dot of buttercream.

Claws and tail: Flatten little balls of light brown fondant for paw pads and tiny, pointed shapes for claws. Roll a thin sausage shape of light brown fondant, about 3 inches long and tapering at one end, for each tail. Secure in place with buttercream, adding a piece of dark brown fondant for the tail ends.

Witch

Ingredients

- 3 oz black rolled fondant
- Confectioners' sugar, for dusting
- 4 gingerbread cookies
- Vanilla buttercream (see page 8)
- 3 oz purple rolled fondant
- 4 oz gray rolled fondant
- Small lilac-colored candies
- Orange food coloring
- Small piece of white rolled fondant
- Small piece of red rolled fondant
- 4 chocolate mint sticks and shredded wheat for broomsticks

Equipment

- Parchment paper, for tracing
- Pencil
- Scissors
- Rolling pin
- Craft knife
- Small spatula
- Paintbrush
- Paper pastry bag (see page 13)

Boots: Trace and cut out the Witch's boots templates (see page 127). Roll out half the black fondant on a surface dusted with confectioners' sugar until about $^1/_{16}$ inch thick. Cut around the templates, and repeat to give 4 of each boot. Secure in place with a little buttercream.

Dress: Using a spatula, spread buttercream over the body area of each gingerbread cookie. Roll out the purple fondant until about $^1/_{16}$ inch thick and cut out 4 rectangles, about $3^1/_2$ x $1^3/_4$ inches. Cut "ragged" edges along one short side of each and place on the cookies so the ragged edge sits over the boots.

Cloak: Trace and cut out the Witch's cloak templates (see page 127). Roll out the gray fondant until about $^1/_{16}$ inch thick and cut around the cloak templates. Repeat to give 4 of each and secure in place with a little buttercream. Add small, purple "patches" on one side, securing with a dampened paintbrush.

Hat: Trace and cut out the Witch's hat template (see opposite). Roll out the remaining black fondant and cut around the template. Repeat to give 4 hats. Secure in place with buttercream. (To hold the point of each hat level, you might need to add an extra piece of black fondant underneath.) Decorate each hat with a candy slice and a strip of purple fondant.

Hair: Beat orange food coloring into the remaining buttercream, adding a little at a time until the desired shade is reached. Put in a paper pastry bag and snip off the merest tip. Use to pipe hair.

Face: Flatten small balls of white fondant for eyes and make hooked noses in red fondant. Roll tiny pieces of red fondant under your fingertips and mold into "zig-zag" shapes for crooked mouths. Secure the features in place with piped buttercream.

Finishing touches: Pipe orange "stitches" around the patches and secure a candy slice to each boot. For the broomsticks, secure blobs of fondant trimmings to the ends of chocolate mint sticks. Cut lengths of shredded wheat cereal and press gently into the fondant. Wrap strips of black fondant around the shredded wheat. Secure to the hands with buttercream.

Spaceboy

Ingredients

- 3 oz blue rolled fondant
- Confectioners' sugar, for dusting
- 4 gingerbread cookies
- 1 oz green rolled fondant
- Tube of white decorator frosting
- Royal icing (see page 9)
- Small piece of yellow rolled fondant
- Small piece of black rolled fondant
- Tube of milk chocolate decorator frosting (or chocolate hazelnut spread or melted milk chocolate)

Equipment

- Rolling pin
- Craft knife
- Paintbrush
- Toothpick
- Parchment paper, for tracing
- Pencil
- Scissors
- Paper pastry bag (optional)

Space suit: Roll out a little of the blue fondant on a surface dusted with confectioners' sugar until about $\frac{1}{16}$ inch thick and cut into 4 thin strips. Fit a strip across the middle of each gingerbread cookie, securing with a little decorator frosting.

Roll the green fondant into a thin band, cut into 8 lengths, and secure across each ankle with a dampened paintbrush.

Use white decorator frosting to pipe an outline around the edge of each cookie, taking the line across each neck and a further line across the wrists. Add a $\frac{3}{4}$-inch square of piping above the belt. Spoon soft white royal icing (see page 16) into all the outlined areas except the hands, spreading the icing into the corners with a toothpick.

Add small rectangles of yellow fondant below the chins on the chests, marking lines with a craft knife. Shape and position 4 small balls of green fondant in the center of each space suit, securing with a dampened paintbrush.

Helmet: Trace and cut out the Spaceboy's helmet template (see opposite). Thinly roll out the remaining blue fondant and cut around the template. Repeat to give 4 helmets. Secure in place with a little decorator frosting.

Face: Add small rounds of black fondant for eyes and piped frosting mouths.

Hair: Use a tube of milk chocolate decorator frosting to pipe hair. (Alternatively, use a little chocolate hazelnut spread or melted milk chocolate in a paper pastry bag.) Use a little more chocolate to pipe a dot on each of the green balls on the space suit.

Alien Girl

Ingredients

- 4 gingerbread cookies
- 7 oz green rolled fondant
- Confectioners' sugar, for dusting
- 2 oz milk chocolate, melted (see page 10)
- Royal icing (see page 9)
- Small piece of blue rolled fondant
- 2 oz dark green rolled fondant
- Tube of white decorator frosting
- Small piece of yellow rolled fondant

Equipment

- Toothpicks
- Craft knife
- Rolling pin
- Gingerbread cutter
- $1^3/_4$- and $1^1/_4$-inch round cutters
- Small star and moon cutters (optional)
- Paper pastry bag (see page 13)

Antenna: The antennae are best fixed when the gingerbread cookies come out of the oven and are still soft. Take half a wooden toothpick and gently press into the top of each cookie until secure enough to stay in place. Allow to cool before decorating.

Shape 4 little strips of green fondant, flattening at one end, and press a strip onto each toothpick. If the fondant doesn't stay in place, dampen the toothpicks with water and try again.

Body: Roll out the green fondant on a surface dusted with confectioners' sugar until about $^1/_{16}$ inch thick. Cut out 4 gingerbread shapes with the cutter, trimming off the hand and feet areas. Using round cutters, cut $1^3/_4$-inch circles out of the centers and $1^1/_4$-inch circles out of the heads. Secure in place on each cookie with blobs of melted chocolate.

Tummy: Spoon soft white royal icing (see page 16) into the large circle removed by the cutter. Cut out little stars and crescents (using cutters or a craft knife) in blue fondant and position over the royal icing.

Hands and feet: Shape dark green fondant into hands and feet and secure with blobs of melted chocolate.

Face: Pipe eye and mouth shapes onto the faces with white decorator frosting. Add small rounds of blue fondant to the eyes and a little melted chocolate to the mouths.

Hair and ribbons: Put the melted chocolate in a pastry bag and snip off the merest tip. Use to pipe chocolate on either side of the faces to resemble hair in "bunches." Add thin strips of yellow fondant for the bows while the chocolate is still soft. Secure large yellow fondant stars to the hands with melted chocolate.

Superhero Boy

Ingredients

- Vanilla buttercream (see page 8)
- 4 gingerbread cookies
- 4 oz blue rolled fondant
- Confectioners' sugar, for dusting
- 2 oz red rolled fondant
- 2 oz dark red rolled fondant
- Tube of black decorator frosting
- Small piece of yellow rolled fondant
- Red icing pen or food coloring

Equipment

- Small spatula
- Rolling pin
- Gingerbread cutter
- Craft knife
- Paintbrush

Costume: Using a spatula, spread a little buttercream over each gingerbread cookie, leaving the hands, feet, and head uncovered. For each suit, roll out a quarter of the blue fondant on a surface dusted with confectioners' sugar until about $1/16$ inch thick. Cut out 4 gingerbread shapes with the cutter, trimming off the fondant at the neck, wrists, and tops of the legs. Secure in place on each cookie.

Roll out the red fondant until about $1/16$ inch thick and cut out triangular shapes, about $2^1/2$ inches wide, for the pants. Secure in place with a dampened paintbrush. Cut out rectangles measuring about $3/4$ x $1/2$ inch for socks. Spread a little buttercream over the gingerbread legs and secure the socks in place.

Cape: Roll out the dark red fondant until about $1/16$ inch thick and cut out 8 curved pieces, each measuring about 1 x $1/2$ inch. Secure 2 around each of the necks for the top of the cape, as in the picture. Cut out 8 rectangles, each about 2 x $3/4$ inches, and then taper them so that they are narrower at the top ends. Secure to the sides of the cookies with a little buttercream.

Hair: Pipe lines of black decorator frosting for the hair.

Face: Use more black decorator frosting to pipe the eyes. Cut red fondant trimmings to make the mouths and secure in place with dots of buttercream.

Finishing touches: Use black decorator frosting to pipe around the edges of the feet. Cut out a triangle of yellow fondant and secure to the front of the costume with a dampened paintbrush. Paint a simple pattern or a child's initial onto the yellow fondant using a red icing pen or food coloring.

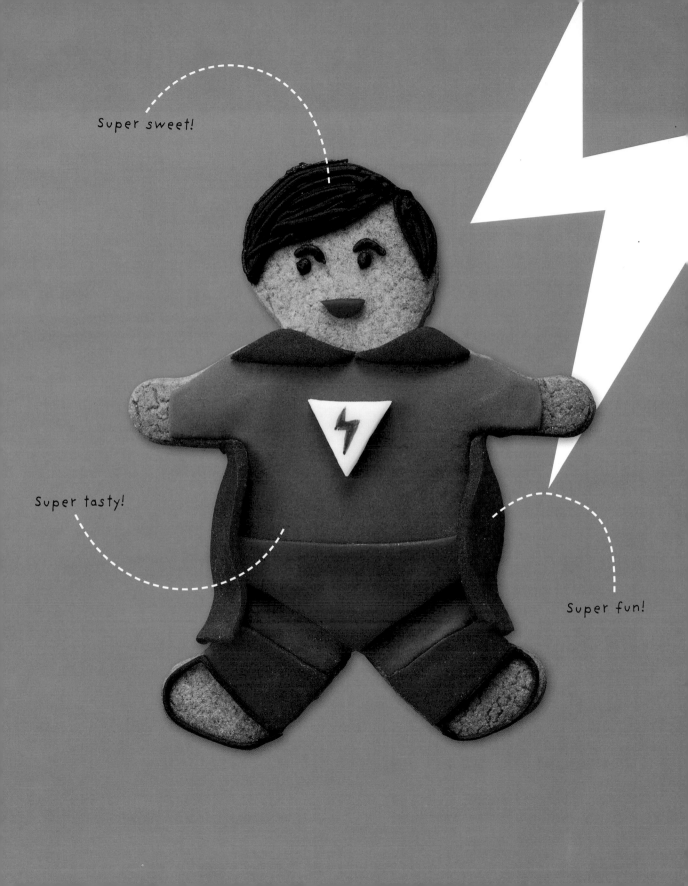

Superhero Girl

Ingredients

- 2 oz red rolled fondant
- Confectioners' sugar, for dusting
- Vanilla buttercream (see page 8)
- 4 gingerbread cookies
- 1½ oz white rolled fondant
- 2 oz blue rolled fondant
- Edible gold food coloring
- Tube of white decorator frosting

Equipment

- Parchment paper, for tracing
- Pencil
- Scissors
- Rolling pin
- Craft knife
- Small spatula
- Paintbrush
- Toothpick
- Gingerbread cutter
- Paper pastry bag (see page 13)

Costume: Trace and cut out the Superhero Girl's bodice and skirt templates (see opposite). Roll out the red fondant on a surface dusted with confectioners' sugar until about ¹/₁₆ inch thick. Cut around the template. Repeat to give 4 bodices. Using a spatula, spread a little buttercream over each of the gingerbread cookie and secure the bodices gently in place.

Roll out long white strips of white fondant, about ¼ inch wide, and fit just below the bodices, securing to the lower edges of the red fondant with a dampened paintbrush and trimming off the excess at the sides.

Thinly roll out the blue fondant and cut around the skirt template. Repeat to give 4 skirts and secure below the white strips. Make folds along the lower edges of the skirts by lifting the fondant at intervals with a toothpick and pinching the fondant around the toothpick so the folds are held in place.

Boots: Spread the feet of each cookie with a little buttercream. For each pair of boots, thinly roll out a quarter of the remaining red fondant. Press each leg of the gingerbread cutter into the fondant, trimming off the top edge in an inverted "v" shape. Cut out deep notches for high heels and secure in place.

Hair: Put the remaining buttercream in a paper pastry bag and snip off the merest tip. Use to pipe long curly hair.

Face: Roll 8 tiny balls of blue fondant for eyes. Secure in place with dots of buttercream, then pipe eyebrows. Use red fondant trimmings to shape each mouth and secure with a dot of white decorator frosting.

Finishing touches:

Cut 8 wide bangle shapes in white fondant and secure to the arms. Cut out 4 triangular shapes for headpieces and press gently into position. Once fairly dry, these can be painted gold. Pipe dots of white decorator frosting onto each skirt, then use to pipe a necklace and trim on the boots.

Deep Sea Diver

Ingredients

- Vanilla buttercream (see page 8)
- 4 gingerbread cookies
- 5 oz gray rolled fondant
- Confectioners' sugar, for dusting
- Small piece of red rolled fondant
- 1 oz blue rolled fondant
- Small piece of black rolled fondant
- 2 oz yellow rolled fondant
- Black food coloring
- Tubes of white and black decorator frosting
- 4 small candies
- 4 strawberry-flavor licorice laces
- Edible gold food coloring (optional)

Equipment

- Small spatula
- Rolling pin
- Gingerbread cutter
- Craft knife
- Paintbrush
- Parchment paper, for tracing
- Pencil
- Scissors

Diving suit: Using a spatula, thinly spread buttercream over each gingerbread cookie. For each diving suit, roll out a quarter of the gray fondant on a surface dusted with confectioners' sugar until about $1/16$ inch thick. Cut out 4 gingerbread shapes with the cutter, trimming off the fondant halfway down the legs. Secure in place on each cookie.

Roll out the red fondant until about $1/16$ inch thick and cut out 4 strips, about $2\frac{1}{2} \times 1/4$ inch. Secure across the waists using a dampened paintbrush.

Boots: For each pair of boots, roll out a quarter of the blue fondant until about $1/16$ inch thick. Press each leg of the gingerbread cutter into the fondant, trimming off the top edge in a straight line halfway up the legs. Secure in place with a dampened paintbrush. Roll out the black fondant to about $1/16$ inch thick and cut out 8 rectangles, about $1 \times 1/4$ inch. Secure one across the bottom of each boot.

Helmet: Trace and cut out the Deep Sea Diver's helmet template (see opposite). Thinly roll out the yellow fondant and cut around the template. Repeat to give 4 helmets. Secure in place with a dampened paintbrush. Mark a line on either side of the helmet, and about $1/4$ inch away from the lower edges with a craft knife. Press the handle end of the paintbrush into the fondant, between the marked line and edges of the helmets, to make a row of indentations, as in the picture.

Face: Paint eyes and mouths onto the gray fondant using black food coloring. Use white decorator frosting to pipe diagonal lines across the face areas and then across in the opposite direction.

Finishing touches: Secure a candy in the center of each belt. Pipe the body straps and wrists using black decorator frosting. If desired, the helmets can be painted with edible gold food coloring. Wrap a strawberry licorice lace around each diver.

Shark

Ingredients

- Vanilla buttercream (see page 8)
- 4 gingerbread cookies
- 5 oz blue rolled fondant
- Confectioners' sugar, for dusting
- 2 oz pale blue rolled fondant
- Small piece of gray rolled fondant
- Small piece of white rolled fondant
- Black food coloring
- Tube of white decorator frosting

Equipment

- Small spatula
- Rolling pin
- Gingerbread cutter
- Craft knife
- Paintbrush

Body: Using a spatula, thinly spread buttercream over each gingerbread cookie, leaving the arms and legs uncovered. Roll out the blue fondant on a surface dusted with confectioners' sugar until about $1/16$ inch thick. Cut out 4 gingerbread shapes with the cutter, trimming off the arms into fin shapes and each leg so the lower edge forms a point. Cut off the fondant at the foot of each left leg. Secure in place on each cookie.

Roll out a little pale blue fondant and trim to fit the body area of the cookie. Secure in position with a dampened paintbrush.

Tail: Cut out 4 tails from the rolled out blue fondant trimmings and secure to the ends of the shark bodies with a dampened paintbrush, curving them up and over the bodies as in the picture.

Face: Roll out the gray fondant until about $1/16$ inch thick and cut out "smiling" mouths. Position tiny balls of white fondant for eyes. Secure the features in place with a dampened paintbrush. Paint the eyes black with food coloring and add eyebrows. Use white decorator frosting to pipe teeth.

Inuit

Ingredients

- 1 tablespoon cocoa powder
- 1 teaspoon boiling water
- Triple quantity vanilla buttercream (see page 8)
- 4 gingerbread cookies
- 2 oz milk chocolate, melted (see page 10)
- Small piece of black rolled fondant
- Confectioners' sugar, for dusting
- Tubes of black and red decorator frosting

Equipment

- Small spatula
- 2 paper pastry bags (see page 13)
- Small star tip
- Craft knife

Coat and pants: Beat the cocoa powder and boiling water into a third of the buttercream. Using a spatula, spread chocolate buttercream over each gingerbread cookie, leaving the heads and feet uncovered. Put the melted chocolate in a paper pastry bag and snip off the merest tip. Use to pipe diagonal lines, about $1/4$ inch apart, over the chocolate buttercream, then across in the opposite direction, leaving the hands unpiped.

Boots: Spread a little vanilla buttercream over the gingerbread feet. Put the remaining vanilla buttercream in a paper pastry bag fitted with a star tip. Use to pipe lines across the tops of the boots.

Fur trim: Use the vanilla buttercream to pipe around the edges of each face, then down the fronts of the coats and across the tops of the legs. Pipe more buttercream across the wrists.

Face and hair: Roll out the black fondant on a surface dusted with confectioners' sugar until about $1/16$ inch thick. Cut out 4 small semicircles of black fondant, each about $1 1/4$ inches across, and cut out notches using a craft knife. Push gently into the buttercream for hair. Pipe eyes and mouths using black and red decorator frosting.

Finishing touch: Pipe thin straps of milk chocolate across the boots.

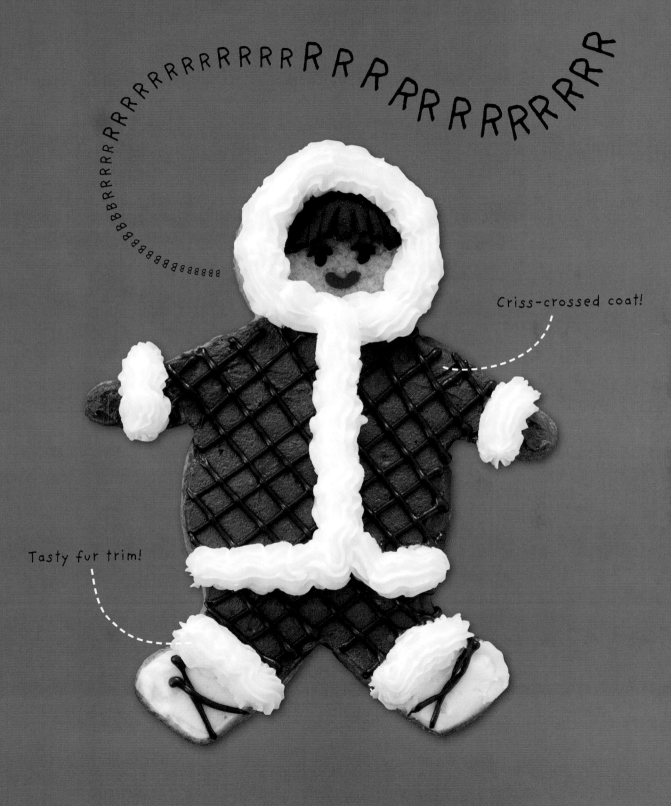

BBBBBRRRRRRRRRRRRRRRRRRRRRRRRRRRRRRRRRRRRR

Criss-crossed coat!

Tasty fur trim!

Look who's come in from the cold...

Penguin

Ingredients

- 3 oz black rolled fondant
- Confectioners' sugar, for dusting
- 3 oz white chocolate, melted (see page 10)
- 4 gingerbread cookies
- Tube of black decorator frosting
- Small piece of pale blue rolled fondant
- $1^1/_2$ oz orange rolled fondant

Equipment

- Parchment paper, for tracing
- Pencil
- Scissors
- Rolling pin
- Craft knife
- Small spatula

Body: Trace and cut out the Penguin's costume templates (see opposite and page 127). Roll out the black fondant on a surface dusted with confectioners' sugar until about $1/_{16}$ inch thick. Cut around the body templates and repeat to give 4 of each.

Using a spatula, spread a thin layer of melted white chocolate over each gingerbread cookie, leaving the hands, feet, and edges of the bodies uncovered. Secure the body pieces gently in place. Reroll the trimmings and cut around the head template. Repeat to give 4 heads. Secure in place.

Face: For the eyes, pipe large circles in black decorator frosting, adding balls of pale blue fondant for the centers. Pipe black dots onto the fondant for pupils. Shape small "beaks" using orange fondant and press gently into the chocolate.

Flippers: For each flipper, flatten a ball of orange fondant to an oval shape about 1 inch long. Cut a slice off one end and mark indentations with a craft knife at the other end. Secure in place with melted chocolate.

try me too! page 42

Pointy beak!

Flipping fantastic!

Who else is taking a dip?

Surfer Dude

Ingredients

- Vanilla buttercream (see page 8)
- 4 gingerbread cookies
- Blue and yellow food coloring
- Pink dragees
- Tube of black decorator frosting
- 4 small mints
- 3 oz pale blue rolled fondant
- Confectioners' sugar, for dusting
- Yellow icing pen or food coloring (optional)

Equipment

- 3 paper pastry bags (see page 13)
- Small spatula
- Rolling pin
- Craft knife
- Paintbrush

Shorts: Put a little of the buttercream in a paper pastry bag and snip off the merest tip. Use to pipe a curved line across the center of each gingerbread cookie and across the legs to define the "shorts" area. Put all but 6 tablespoons of the remaining buttercream in a bowl and beat in blue food coloring, adding a little at a time until the desired shade is reached. Using a spatula, spread the buttercream over the shorts area of each cookie. Pipe vanilla buttercream bows at the front.

Color 2 tablespoons of the buttercream bright yellow and put in a paper pastry bag. Snip off the merest tip and use to pipe circles of dots over the shorts to make simple flower shapes. Press pink dragees into the centers. Pipe squiggles of vanilla buttercream and yellow buttercream dots between the flowers.

Chest: Use the vanilla buttercream to pipe a "6 pack" chest on each gingerbread.

Hair: Color 2 tablespoons of the buttercream light yellow to pipe long wavy hair. Pipe vanilla buttercream across the top of the hair for a headband.

Face: Color the last 2 tablespoons of buttercream pale blue. Put in a paper pastry bag and snip off the merest tip. Use the vanilla and blue buttercreams to pipe the eyes. Use a line of vanilla buttercream for teeth and then outline with red decorator frosting.

Finishing touches: Use black decorator frosting, and any other colors you prefer, to pipe necklaces and wrist bands. Press a small mint into the center of each necklace.

Surf board: Roll out the pale blue fondant on a surface dusted with confectioners' sugar until about $1/16$ inch thick. Cut out 4 surf board shapes, each about $5\frac{1}{2}$ inches long, and cut straight across at the base. Allow to harden for several hours on parchment paper. Paint a simple design onto the surf boards, using either a yellow icing pen or diluted yellow food coloring and a fine paintbrush.

Hula Dancer

try me too! page 52

Ingredients

- Vanilla buttercream (see page 8)
- 4 gingerbread cookies
- Soft green and yellow gummy candies
- Blue food coloring
- Pink and white dragees
- 2 tablespoons chocolate hazelnut spread
- Tube of red decorator frosting

Equipment

- Small spatula
- Craft knife
- 3 paper pastry bags (see page 13)
- Small star tip

Grass skirt: Using a spatula, spread a thin layer of buttercream over the skirt area of each gingerbread cookie. Cut plenty of soft green and yellow gummy candies into pieces and press down gently into the buttercream, starting with a row around the lower edge of the skirt and building it up in layers. Put about 1 tablespoon buttercream in a paper pastry bag and snip off the merest tip. Use to pipe a decorative edge of buttercream along the top of the candies, which should come slightly below waist level. Pipe a little belly button above each skirt.

Flower garland and bracelets: Beat blue food coloring into the remaining buttercream, adding a little at a time until the desired shade is reached. Put in a paper pastry bag fitted with a star tip. Use to pipe flower garlands around the neck of each cookie, and around one of the wrists and one of the ankles. Press small colored pink and white dragees into the garlands.

Hair: Put the chocolate hazelnut spread in a paper pastry bag and snip off the merest tip. Use to pipe long wavy hair. For each cookie, decorate the hair with a small flower by piping a large blob of blue buttercream and pressing a pink dragee into the center.

Face: Use the vanilla buttercream and chocolate hazelnut spread to pipe eyes. Add small mouths using red decorator frosting.

Dinosaur

Ingredients

- Vanilla buttercream (see page 8)
- 4 gingerbread cookies
- 5 oz green rolled fondant
- Confectioners' sugar, for dusting
- Small piece of yellow rolled fondant
- Tube of yellow decorator frosting
- Small piece of chocolate-flavored or brown rolled fondant
- Small piece of white rolled fondant
- Brown food coloring

Equipment

- Small spatula
- Rolling pin
- Gingerbread cutter
- Craft knife
- Paintbrush

Body: Using a spatula, spread a thin layer of buttercream over each gingerbread cookie, leaving the tummy areas and arms uncovered. Roll out the green fondant on a surface dusted with confectioners' sugar until about $1/16$ inch thick, and cut out 4 gingerbread shapes with the cutter (rerolling the trimmings, if necessary, to make enough shapes). Trim off the arms and cut out a large oval shape from each center. Cut out small notches from the feet. Secure in place on each cookie.

Roll tiny balls of yellow fondant between your finger and thumb. Flatten slightly and press into the green fondant, as in the picture. Pipe lines across the tummy areas using yellow decorator frosting, then pipe claws onto the feet.

Arms: Shape thin arms, about $3/4$ inch long, in green fondant and secure in place with buttercream. Roll pea-size balls of green fondant, flatten slightly, and cut three slits into each. Position at the end of the arms. Add claws using yellow decorator frosting.

Face: For each cookie, shape a horn using chocolate-flavored or brown fondant and secure to the top of each head with a dampened paintbrush. Add balls of white fondant for eyes, adding semicircles of green fondant for eyelids. Paint the eyes brown using a little diluted brown food coloring. Use the end of a paintbrush or skewer to indent 2 nostrils. Indent a long thin mouth with the tip of a craft knife and pipe 2 fangs with yellow decorator frosting.

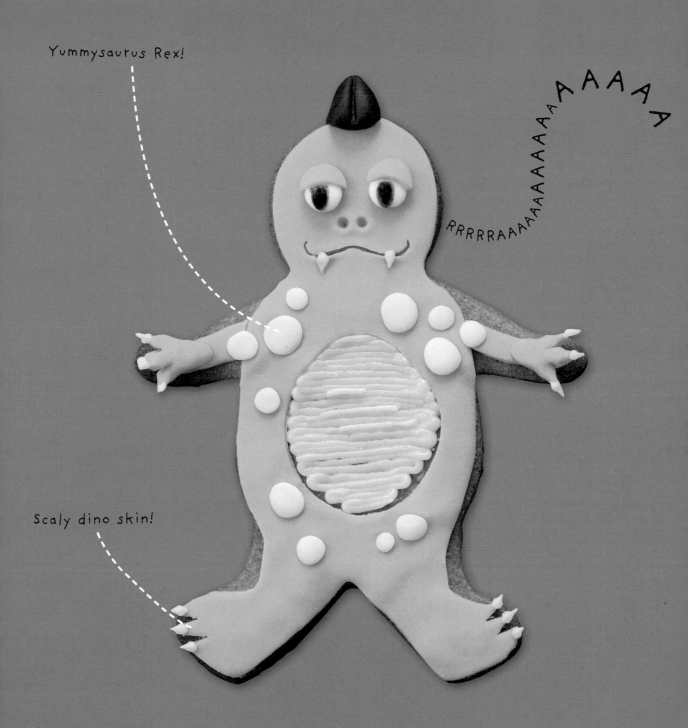

Yummysaurus Rex!

RRRRRAAAAAAAAAAAAAAAAAA

Scaly dino skin!

See who's next for lunch... 👉

Explorer

Ingredients

- Vanilla buttercream (see page 8)
- 4 gingerbread cookies
- 3 oz cream-colored rolled fondant
- Confectioners' sugar, for dusting
- 4 small square candies
- Small piece of chocolate-flavored or brown rolled fondant
- Small piece of green rolled fondant
- Tube of red decorator frosting
- 8 small round candies
- 4 chocolate mint sticks

Equipment

- Small spatula
- Rolling pin
- Craft knife
- Paper pastry bag (see page 13)

Shorts: Using a spatula, spread a little buttercream over the shorts area of each gingerbread cookie. For each pair of shorts, roll out a little cream-colored fondant on a surface dusted with confectioners' sugar until about $1/16$ inch thick and cut out a rectangle measuring about $2^1/2$ x $1^3/4$ inches. Cut a little triangle out of the lower edge and press gently into position on each cookie.

Put the remaining buttercream in a paper pastry bag and snip off the merest tip. Use to pipe belts around the tops and the shorts details, as in the picture. Roll and cut out long thin strips of cream-colored fondant, about $1/8$ inch wide. Cut across into $1/2$-inch lengths and secure over the belts as belt carriers. Add a small square candy for each buckle.

Boots: Mold boot shapes from chocolate-flavored or brown fondant and secure in place with buttercream. Pipe lines of buttercream above the boots for socks.

Shirt and backpack: Pipe "shirt" outlines over the top half of each cookie, adding several pocket shapes. Roll out thin strips of brown fondant and secure over the shoulders for backpack straps.

Scarf: Roll out the remaining brown fondant to a long thin strip. Roll very thin lengths of green fondant under your fingertips. Space lengths $1/4$ inch apart over the brown fondant. Roll with a rolling pin until the two fondants are flattened together. Cut $3/4$-inch wide strips from this and secure around each neck for a scarf.

Hat and goggles: Roll out the cream-colored fondant trimmings and cut out 4 semicircular shapes for the hats, each measuring $1^3/4$ inches across. Secure in place with buttercream.

For the goggles, pipe a line of buttercream around the brim of each hat and place 2 small candies at the center. Pipe circles of buttercream onto the candies.

Face: Pipe buttercream eyes and press small balls of brown fondant into the centers. Pipe small round mouths using red decorator frosting.

Butterfly net: Secure flat, semicircular pieces of chocolate-flavored or brown fondant to the ends of the chocolate mint sticks. Pipe lines of buttercream, first in one direction, then the other, onto the fondant to resemble netting. Secure in place.

Cowboy

Ingredients

- Tubes of black, red, and white decorator frosting
- 4 gingerbread cookies
- 2 oz milk chocolate, melted (see page 10)
- 4 small chocolate-flavored candies
- 12 chocolate mints
- 2 raisins
- 8 small chocolate cake decorating balls, or candies
- 1 strawberry-flavor licorice lace

Equipment

- Small spatula
- Craft knife
- Parchment paper, for tracing
- Pencil
- Scissors

Vest: Use black decorator frosting to pipe the outline of a vest onto each gingerbread cookie. Fill in the shapes with more piping.

Neckerchief: Pipe triangular shapes at the necks using red decorator frosting. Fill in the areas with more red piping. Pipe white dots of decorator frosting over the red frosting.

Pants: Using a spatula, spread the chocolate over the pants area of each cookie. Pipe belts using black decorator frosting, adding small chocolate candies for buckles.

Hat and boots: Trace and cut out the Cowboy's hat and boots templates (see opposite). Position the hat template over one of the chocolate mints and cut around with a craft knife. Repeat to give 4 hats. Cut out the boots in the same way. Secure in place with melted chocolate. Pipe an outline around the edge of each chocolate shape using black decorator frosting.

Face and hair: Cut the raisins in half and secure in place with decorator frosting for mouths. Secure the chocolate balls for eyes. Pipe black decorator frosting around the edges for hair.

Lasso: Curl up lengths of strawberry lace and secure to the hands with red decorator frosting. (You might need to hold these in place for a while until each lasso keeps its shape.)

Native American Girl

Ingredients

- Tubes of red, yellow, white, and black decorator frosting
- 4 gingerbread cookies
- 4 small flat strawberry licorices, or other red chewy candies
- 2 raisins
- 8 small chocolate cake decorating balls, or candies

Equipment

- Craft knife

Dress: Using red and yellow decorator frosting, pipe a "v" shape neckline, sleeves, belt, and hemline onto each gingerbread cookie. Use more yellow and white decorator frosting to pipe rows of $3/4$-inch vertical lines down from both the necklines and hems.

Hair and headdress: Use black decorator frosting to pipe long hair. Pipe 2 curved lines of red frosting across each forehead. Use a craft knife to cut out curved "feather" shapes from the strawberry licorices. Cut out notches around the edges. Press gently into the black frosting. Pipe bands of red frosting over the pigtails, as in the picture.

Face: Cut the raisins in half and secure in place with decorator frosting for mouths. Secure the chocolate balls for eyes.

Moccasins: Use yellow and white decorator frosting to pipe slender moccasins, adding a dot of red decorating frosting to each for the red pompoms.

try me too! page 118

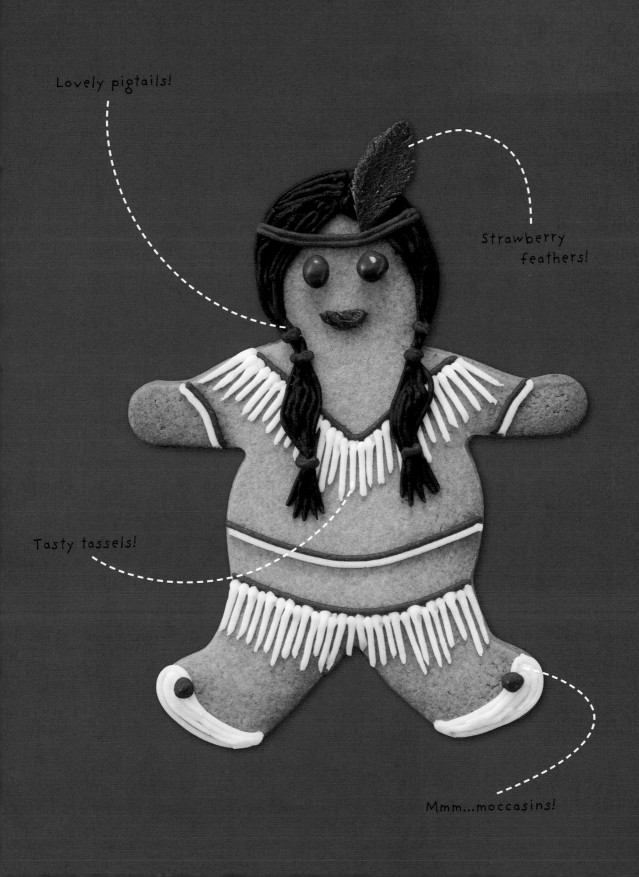

Lovely pigtails!

Strawberry feathers!

Tasty tassels!

Mmm...moccasins!

Doctor

Ingredients

- Tubes of white, green, yellow, and red decorator frosting
- 4 gingerbread cookies
- Royal icing (see page 9)
- Mini chocolate chips
- 1 thin white chewy candy in any flavor
- 2 tablespoons chocolate hazelnut spread
- 1 soft strawberry-flavor licorice
- 2 strawberry-flavor licorice laces
- 4 small round candies

Equipment

- Toothpick
- Scissors
- Paper pastry bag (see page 13)

White coat: Use white decorator frosting to pipe a coat outline onto the body of each gingerbread cookie, taking the line across the cuffs, tops of the legs, and to a "v" shape at the neck. Spoon soft white royal icing (see page 16) into the outlined areas, spreading the icing into the corners with a toothpick. Allow to set for about an hour before piping collar outlines, pockets, and cuffs with white decorator frosting. Position 4 mini chocolate chips down the front of each coat, securing in place with dots of decorator frosting. Add tiny dots of decorator frosting for buttonholes.

Shirt and tie: Using scissors, cut 8 small diamond shapes from a thin white chewy candy and secure 2 at the neck of each cookie with a dot of decorator frosting to shape the shirt collar. Pipe striped ties in contrasting colors of decorator frosting such as green and yellow.

Hair: Pipe squiggles of hair at each side of the head using white decorator frosting.

Face: Put a little chocolate hazelnut spread in a paper pastry bag and snip off the merest tip. Use to pipe small blobs for noses. Add eyes by piping large blobs of white decorator frosting, finishing with chocolate spread centers. Shape mouths by cutting small semicircles of strawberry licorice and securing with decorator frosting. Secure a double width of strawberry lace across each forehead, positioning a small candy in the center of each.

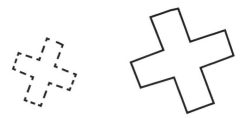

Shoes: Use a little chocolate hazelnut spread to pipe the outlines of shoes, then fill in the centers with more piping.

Stethoscope: Cut short lengths of strawberry lace and secure two ends at the shoulders with red decorator frosting. Pipe a blob of red frosting onto the coats to secure the laces at the other ends.

Nurse

Ingredients

- Blue food coloring
- Royal icing (see page 9)
- 4 gingerbread cookies
- 2 tablespoons chocolate hazelnut spread
- Several thin white chewy candies in any flavor
- Red icing pen (optional)
- Tubes of red and white decorator frosting

Equipment

- 2 paper pastry bags (see page 13)
- Toothpick
- Scissors

Dress: Beat blue food coloring into the royal icing, adding a little at a time until the desired shade is reached. Put about a quarter into a paper pastry bag and snip off the merest tip. Use to pipe an outline onto the body of each gingerbread cookie, taking the line across the cuffs, tops of the legs, and finish with a curved edge at the neck. Spoon the remaining royal icing (see page 16) into the outlined areas, spreading the icing into the corners with a toothpick.

Hair: Put a little chocolate hazelnut spread in a paper pastry bag and snip off the merest tip. Use to pipe hair.

Apron and headpiece: Using scissors, cut out rectangles of various sizes from thin white chewy candies. Press gently in place for the aprons, collars, and headpieces while the icing is still soft. As a guide, the 8 collar rectangles should measure about $3/4$ x $1/4$ inch, the 4 lower parts of each apron about $1^1/2$ x 1 inches, the 4 tops of each apron about $1^1/4$ x $3/4$ inches (these can be tapered slightly at the sides), and the 4 headpieces also about $1^1/4$ x $3/4$ inches. If desired, cut a curved top edge to the headpieces. Use a red icing pen or red decorator frosting to pipe small red crosses.

Face: Use white decorator frosting to pipe eyes and noses, and red decorator frosting to pipe mouths.

Shoes: Use white decorator frosting to pipe the outlines of shoes, then fill in with more piping.

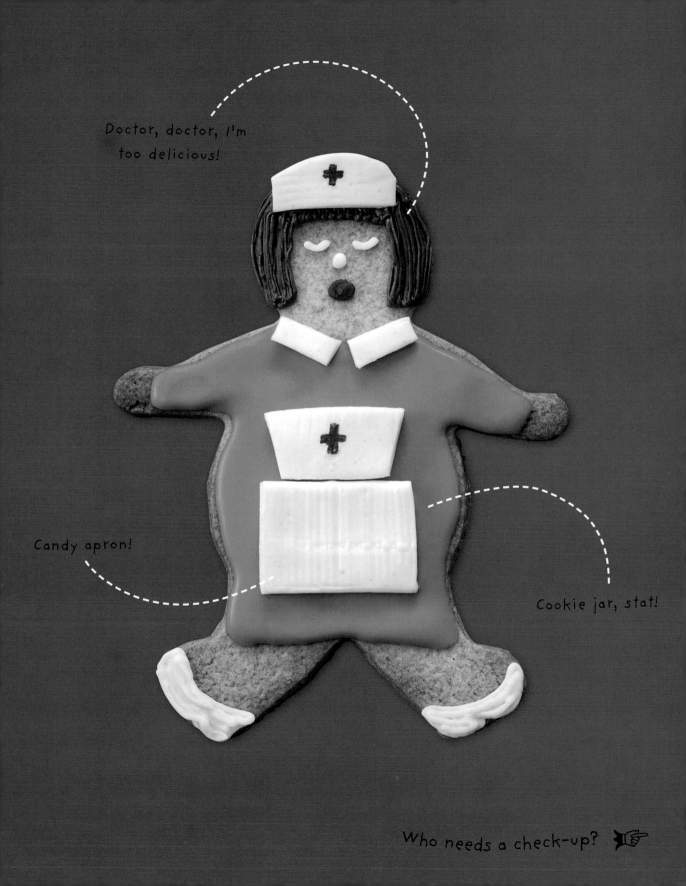

Soccer Star

Ingredients

- 3 oz red rolled fondant
- Confectioners' sugar, for dusting
- Vanilla buttercream (see page 8)
- 4 gingerbread cookies
- $2^1/_2$ oz white rolled fondant
- White, black, and yellow decorator frosting
- 1 teaspoon cocoa powder
- Small piece of blue rolled fondant

Equipment

- Small spatula
- Rolling pin
- Gingerbread cutter
- Craft knife
- Paper pastry bag (see page 13)

Shirt and shorts: Using a spatula, spread a little vanilla buttercream over the body area of each gingerbread cookie. For each shirt, roll out a quarter of the red fondant on a surface dusted with confectioners' sugar until about $3^1/_4$ inches in diameter and about $1/_{16}$ inch thick. Cut out the shirt area of the gingerbread body with the cutter. Cut a "v" shape at the neck and trim off the fondant at the sleeves and across the waist. Secure in place.

For each pair of shorts, roll out a quarter of the white fondant until about $2^3/_4$ inches in diameter and about $1/_{16}$ inch thick. Cut out a pair of white shorts in the same way as the shirt. Secure in place.

Use white decorator frosting to pipe white trim around the edges of each shirt. Use all the colors of decorator frosting to pipe a small badge onto each shirt.

Socks: For each pair of socks, roll out the red fondant trimmings until about $1/_{16}$ inch thick and cut out 2 rectangles, each measuring about $1 \times 1/_2$ inch. Secure to the legs with buttercream, then pipe a line of white decorator frosting along the tops.

Boots: Use black decorator frosting to pipe the outlines of boots, adding small dots for studs along the lower edges.

Hair and hair band: Put the remaining buttercream in a small bowl and beat in the cocoa powder. Put in a paper pastry bag and snip off the merest tip. Use to pipe hair, adding a piped line of black frosting around the top to resemble a hair band.

Face: Flatten tiny balls of white fondant trimmings and secure in place with dots of decorator frosting for eyes, adding smaller balls of blue fondant for the centers. Pipe mouths using red decorator frosting.

Ballerina

Ingredients

- Vanilla buttercream (see page 8)
- 4 gingerbread cookies
- 5 oz white rolled fondant
- Confectioners' sugar, for dusting
- 2 oz pale pink rolled fondant
- Brown food coloring
- Pink and white dragees
- $\frac{1}{2}$ oz pale blue rolled fondant
- Tube of red decorator frosting

Equipment

- Small spatula
- 2 paper pastry bags (see page 13)
- Craft knife
- 3- and $1\frac{3}{4}$-inch round cookie cutters
- Toothpick

Tutu: Using a spatula, spread a little buttercream over the lower half of each gingerbread body. Reserve 2 tablespoons of the remaining buttercream and put the rest in a paper pastry bag. Snip off the merest tip.

Roll out a quarter of the white fondant on a surface dusted with confectioners' sugar until about $\frac{1}{16}$ inch thick. Cut out 4 triangles, each measuring $2\frac{1}{2}$ inches along the longest side and $1\frac{3}{4}$ inches along the other sides. Secure in place for knickers. Pipe a line of buttercream along the top edge of each.

Thinly roll out more white fondant and cut out four 3-inch rounds with a cookie cutter. Roll a horizontally held toothpick around the edges of the fondant so that it starts to frill (see page 15). Cut out a $1\frac{3}{4}$-inch circle from the center of each with a cookie cutter, then cut each ring of fondant in half. For each tutu, open out one length of frilled fondant and arrange along the top edge of the knickers, so it's held in place by the piped buttercream. Arrange another piece of frilled fondant on top, securing in place with more buttercream. Pull the frilled edges up with the tip of a toothpick to accentuate a tutu shape.

Using the buttercream, pipe the outline of a dainty top on each cookie. Roll out half the pink fondant and cut out 4 thin strips, about $2\frac{1}{2}$ inches long. Secure one around the waist of each ballerina.

Hair: Beat brown food coloring into the reserved buttercream, adding a little at a time until the desired shade is reached. Put in a paper pastry bag and snip off the merest tip. Use to pipe hair, adding little "bun" shapes at the top. Cut out thin strips of pink fondant and press into position below the buns. Secure rows of pink and white dragees with dots of buttercream.

Face: Flatten 2 small balls of white fondant and secure in place with dots of buttercream for eyes. Add 2 smaller balls of blue fondant for the centers. Pipe circles of red decorator frosting for the mouths and add small balls of pink fondant for the noses.

Shoes: Cut out dainty shoes in pink fondant and secure with buttercream. Pipe "ribbons" of buttercream that come slightly up the legs.

Finishing touches: Roll out the pink fondant trimmings and cut out 8 rectangles, each about $3/4$ x $1/4$ inch. Secure to the wrists with buttercream. Secure a pink dragee to each of the tops with a dot of buttercream.

Baseballer

Ingredients

- Glacé icing (see page 8)
- 4 gingerbread cookies
- 3 oz white rolled fondant
- Confectioners' sugar, for dusting
- 3 oz burgundy rolled fondant
- 1 oz blue rolled fondant
- Tube of black decorator frosting
- 1 candied cherry
- $\frac{1}{2}$ oz black rolled fondant

Equipment

- Small spatula
- Rolling pin
- Gingerbread cutter
- Craft knife
- Paintbrush
- Paper pastry bag (see page 13)
- $1\frac{1}{2}$-inch round cookie cutter

Shirt: Using a spatula, spread a little glacé icing over the shirt area of each gingerbread cookie. Roll out two-thirds of the white fondant on a surface dusted with confectioners' sugar until about $\frac{1}{16}$ inch thick. Roll very thin lengths of burgundy fondant under your fingertips and arrange $\frac{1}{4}$ inch apart over the white fondant. Roll with a rolling pin until the two are flattened together. Cut into 4 pieces.

Cut out a shirt from each piece with the gingerbread cutter. Cut a "v" shape at the neck and trim off the fondant at the sleeves and across the waist. Secure in place.

Roll out long thin strips of burgundy fondant, about $\frac{1}{4}$ inch wide, and secure with a dampened paintbrush at the front and neckline of the shirts. Put a little of the glacé icing in a paper pastry bag and snip off the merest tip. Use to pipe buttons down the fronts.

Pants: Spread a little more glacé icing over the lower half of each cookie. For each pair of pants, thinly roll out a little of the burgundy fondant. Cut out pants shapes with the gingerbread cutter, trimming off the fondant at the waist and ankles. Secure in place, piping a line of white icing across the knees and the outlines of boots.

Cap and hair: Roll out the blue fondant and cut out two $1\frac{1}{2}$-inch rounds with a cookie cutter, then cut each in half. Secure to the tops of the heads with glacé icing. Shape 4 similar size pieces of blue fondant and secure to the front edge of each cap to make a peak. Mark lines on each cap with a craft knife and add a small ball of burgundy icing to the top. Use black decorator frosting to pipe curly hair.

Face: Pipe black frosting eyes and add small pieces of candied cherry for the mouths, securing with a dab of glacé icing.

Gloves: For each glove, take a small ball of white fondant and flatten slightly. Indent fingers and thumb shapes with a craft knife and secure in place with a dot of glacé icing, curving each glove forward slightly.

Baseball bat: Roll out 4 thin lengths of black fondant, each about $2^{3}/_{4}$ inches long and tapering almost to a point at one end. Allow to harden on a piece of parchment paper before securing to the hands with glacé icing.

Cheerleader

Ingredients

- Glacé icing (see page 8)
- 4 gingerbread cookies
- 3 oz pale pink rolled fondant
- Confectioners' sugar, for dusting
- 2 oz dark pink rolled fondant
- 1 oz yellow rolled fondant
- Small piece of burgundy rolled fondant
- 1 oz white rolled fondant
- Small piece of chocolate-flavored or brown rolled fondant
- 1 candied cherry

Equipment

- Small spatula
- Rolling pin
- Craft knife
- Paintbrush
- Parchment paper, for tracing
- Pencil
- Scissors
- Gingerbread cutter

Skirt and top: Using a spatula, spread a little glacé icing over the skirt area of each gingerbread cookie. Roll out the pale pink fondant on a surface dusted with confectioners' sugar until about $1/16$ inch thick. Cut out 4 rectangles, each measuring about $2^1/_2$ x $3/_4$ inches, and secure in place. For each top, shape 2 triangles of pink fondant and secure in place with glacé icing.

Roll long thin strips of dark pink fondant under your fingertips until not much thicker than string and secure to the tops of the skirts and around the necklines with a dampened paintbrush, trimming off the ends to fit. Shape and position a small bow at the center of each top and little triangles on the skirts for pleats, securing in place with a dampened paintbrush.

Hair: Trace and cut out the Cheerleader's hair template (see opposite). Roll out the yellow fondant until about $1/16$ inch thick and cut around the template. Repeat to give 4 sets of hair. Make shallow cuts with the tip of a craft knife and secure in place with glacé icing. Shape and secure hair bands of burgundy fondant at the joins.

Face: Use small balls of white fondant for the eyes, securing in place with glacé icing. Add tiny balls of chocolate-flavored or brown fondant for the centers, securing with a dampened paintbrush. Add small pieces of candied cherry for the mouths.

Boots: Spread the feet of each cookie with glacé icing. For each pair of boots, thinly roll out a quarter of the white fondant. Press each leg of the gingerbread cutter into the fondant, trimming off the top edge in a straight line. Cut out deep notches for high heels and secure in place.

Pompoms: For each pompom, roll out strips of burgundy or pale pink fondant until about $1/16$ inch thick and measuring about $2^3/4$ x $2^1/4$ inches. Make deep cuts all along one long side, keeping the other long edge intact for the handle. Dampen with a paintbrush and roll up to create a pompom. Hold the handle end, letting the cut strips fall around it and place on a sheet of parchment paper to harden. Make more pompoms in the same way. Secure to the hands with glacé icing.

Karate Boy

Ingredients

- Vanilla buttercream (see page 8)
- 4 gingerbread cookies
- 5 oz white rolled fondant
- Confectioners' sugar, for dusting
- Small piece of black rolled fondant
- Small piece of chocolate-flavored or brown rolled fondant
- Small piece of red rolled fondant
- Tubes of black and white decorator frosting

Equipment

- Small spatula
- Rolling pin
- Gingerbread cutter
- Craft knife
- Paintbrush
- Parchment paper, for tracing
- Pencil
- Scissors

Clothing: Using a spatula, spread a little buttercream over the body, arm, and leg areas of each gingerbread cookie, leaving the hands and feet uncovered. For each jacket, roll out 1 oz of the white fondant on a surface dusted with confectioners' sugar until about $1/16$ inch thick. Cut out the jacket area of the gingerbread body with the cutter, trimming off the fondant in a deep "v" shape at the neckline and straight across at the wrists and waist. Secure in place.

For each pair of pants, thinly roll out a quarter of the remaining fondant. Cut out pants shapes with the gingerbread cutter, trimming off the fondant at the waist and ankles. Secure in place.

Reroll the trimmings and for each jacket cut 2 rectangles of white fondant, about $1^1/4$ x $^3/4$ inch. Position below the waist edge of the jacket, overlapping them slightly, and secure with a dampened paintbrush. Use a craft knife to make shallow cuts about $1/4$ inch away from the edges of the cuffs and around the fronts. Roll out a little black fondant and cut out 4 thin strips. Secure around each waist with a dampened paintbrush, adding another small folded strip for the "tie."

Hair and scarf: Trace and cut out the Karate Boy's hair template (see opposite). Thinly roll out the chocolate-flavored or brown fondant and cut around the template. Repeat to give 4 sets of hair. Secure in place with buttercream. Shape and secure a thin strip of red fondant on top of each with a dampened paintbrush, as in the picture, adding molded scarf ends.

Face: Shape eyes using flattened balls of white fondant and secure with buttercream, adding black decorator frosting for the centers. Knead together a little of the red fondant trimmings with the same quantity of white. Roll into little balls and secure for noses. Cut small rectangles of red fondant for the mouths. Pipe a thin line of white decorator frosting across the center of each mouth.

Flip flops: Secure a strip of black fondant to each foot with black decorator frosting, piping a thin line of frosting to the top to resemble flip flops.

Ice Skater

Ingredients

- Vanilla buttercream (see page 8)
- 4 gingerbread cookies
- 4 oz lilac rolled fondant
- Confectioners' sugar, for dusting
- Tubes of white and red decorator frosting
- $1\frac{1}{2}$ oz white rolled fondant
- Edible silver food coloring
- 4 small candies
- Brown food coloring
- Small piece of blue rolled fondant
- Small piece of pink rolled fondant

Equipment

- Small spatula
- Rolling pin
- Gingerbread cutter
- Craft knife
- Writing tip (optional)
- Paintbrush
- $2\frac{3}{4}$-inch round cookie cutter
- Toothpick
- Paper pastry bag

Leotard and skirt: Using a spatula, spread a little buttercream over the body area of each gingerbread cookie, leaving the hands and legs uncovered. For each skater's top, roll out a quarter of the lilac fondant on a surface dusted with confectioners' sugar until about about $\frac{1}{16}$ inch thick. Cut out the top half of the gingerbread body with the cutter. Cut a "v" shape at the neck and trim off the fondant at the wrists and waist. Secure in place. Use the end of a paintbrush handle or the edge of a writing tip to impress a pattern over the fondant.

Thinly roll out the fondant trimmings and cut out two $2\frac{3}{4}$-inch rounds with a cookie cutter, then cut each in half. Roll a toothpick around the outer edges of one semicircle so that it starts to frill (see page 15). Cut out a curve from the inner edge of the frilled semicircle and open out the shape into a skirt. Secure in place with a dampened paintbrush. Repeat with the remaining semicircles.

Use white decorator frosting to pipe lines across the waists and at the necks and cuffs of the leotards.

Boots: Spread the feet of each cookie with buttercream. For each pair of boots, roll out a quarter of the white fondant until about $\frac{1}{16}$ inch thick. Press each leg of the gingerbread cutter into the fondant, trimming off the top edge in a straight line. Secure in place. Cut 2 thin strips of white fondant, each measuring about $1\frac{1}{4}$ x $\frac{1}{8}$ inches. Secure around the bases of the boots with a dampened paintbrush. Pipe laces in white decorator frosting. Paint the "blades" with edible silver food coloring.

Medal: Pipe a ribbon around the neck of each cookie using red decorator frosting. Press a small candy at the end of each. Pipe a number "1" onto each candy.

Hair: Beat brown food coloring into the remaining buttercream, adding a little at a time until the desired shade is reached. Put in a pastry bag and snip of the merest tip. Pipe long wavy hair using black decorator frosting.

Face: Use balls of white fondant for the eyes, securing in place with white decorator frosting. Add small balls of blue fondant for the centers. Add small balls of pink fondant for the noses and smiling mouths in white and red decorator frosting.

Firefighter

Ingredients

- Orange and brown food coloring
- Vanilla buttercream (see page 8)
- 4 gingerbread cookies
- Tubes of black and red decorator frosting
- 4 yellow or orange fruit chews
- 3 oz dark blue rolled fondant
- Confectioners' sugar, for dusting
- 1 licorice wheel
- 4 small yellow candies
- 1 oz yellow rolled fondant
- 4 plain licorice candies

Equipment

- Small spatula
- Craft knife
- Rolling pin
- Gingerbread cutter
- Toothpick
- Parchment paper, for tracing
- Pencil
- Scissors

Pants: Beat orange food coloring into a third of the buttercream, adding a little at a time until the desired shade is reached. Using a spatula, spread the buttercream over the lower half of each gingerbread cookie, leaving the feet uncovered.

Boots: Use black decorator frosting to pipe the outlines of boots, then fill in with more piping. Slice the fruit chews and add strips to the tops of the boots.

Jacket: For each jacket, roll out a quarter of the dark blue fondant on a surface dusted with confectioners' sugar until about $1/16$ inch thick. Cut out the jacket area of the gingerbread body with the cutter, trimming off the fondant at the neckline, wrists, and waist. Secure in place with buttercream.

Reroll the trimmings and for each jacket cut 2 rectangles of blue fondant, about $1^{1}/_{4}$ x $^{3}/_{4}$ inches, and secure below the waist with buttercream, overlapping them slightly. Unroll the licorice wheel and cut 4 strips to the width of the bodies. Secure in place with black decorator frosting, adding a small candy for each buckle. Cut more pieces of the licorice and secure for cuffs. Pipe 2 rows of buttons down the fronts of the jackets using black decorator frosting and a line of black frosting around each neck.

Hair and face: Beat brown food coloring into a little of the remaining buttercream, adding a little at a time until the desired shade is reached. Spread around the sides of each face for hair. Add a blob of orange buttercream for the nose and pipe black decorator frosting for the eyes and eyebrows. Pipe small red mouths using decorator frosting. Using a toothpick, dot a little brown buttercream over the mouths for mustaches.

Helmet: Trace and cut out the Firefighter's helmet template (see right). Roll out the yellow fondant until about $1/16$ inch thick and cut around the template. Repeat to give 4 helmets. Secure in place with buttercream. Pipe 3 vertical lines and a horizontal band onto each helmet using black decorator frosting.

Torch: Wrap a strip of dark blue fondant trimmings around each licorice candy. Secure a flattened piece of yellow fondant to the end and a dot of vanilla buttercream to the side for the switch. Secure to the hands with buttercream.

Chef

Ingredients

- Tubes of white, black, and red decorator frosting
- 4 gingerbread cookies
- Royal icing (see page 9)
- Small piece of brown rolled fondant
- Confectioners' sugar, for dusting
- 4 thin white chewy candies
- Red icing pen or red food coloring

Equipment

- Toothpick
- Parchment paper, for tracing
- Pencil
- Scissors
- Paintbrush (optional)
- Craft knife

Jacket, pants, and shoes: Use white decorator frosting to pipe an outline around the edge of each gingerbread cookie, taking the line across the neck and halfway across each arm. Spoon soft white royal icing (see page 16) into the outlined areas, spreading the icing into the corners with a toothpick. Allow to set for about an hour before piping buttons down the fronts using red decorator frosting.

Use black decorator frosting to pipe lines onto the pants, first in one direction, then across in the other. Fill in alternate squares with black frosting to create a checker pattern.

Hair and face: Use black decorator frosting to pipe hair. Roll balls of brown fondant for noses and secure in place with white decorator frosting. Add mouths in red decorator frosting, and use black decorator frosting to pipe the mustache, eyes, and eyebrows.

Hat: Trace and cut out the Chef's hat template (see opposite). Lay the template over a white chewy sweet and cut around with scissors. Repeat to give 4 hats. Press into position over the hair.

Finishing touches: Use the icing pen or red food coloring and a paintbrush to paint a small emblem or name onto the jackets. For rolling pins, roll thin lengths of brown fondant under your fingertips to a width of about $1/2$ inch. Cut into four 2-inch lengths. Impress a groove at both ends with the back of a craft knife. Secure to the hands with decorator frosting.

Chewy chef's hat!

Scrumptious rolling pin!

Gigantic mustache!

Waitress

Ingredients

- Tubes of white, black, and red decorator frosting
- 4 gingerbread cookies
- 6 thin white chewy candies
- Small piece of yellow rolled fondant

Equipment

- Scissors

Blouse: Use white decorator frosting to pipe the outline of a blouse onto each gingerbread cookie, adding details such as a pocket and decorative trim, as in the picture.

Skirt and apron: Pipe the outline of a skirt onto each cookie using black decorator frosting. Fill in the shapes with vertical lines of piping. Using scissors, cut out small squares, about 1 x 1 inch, from the thin white chewy candies and press gently into the black frosting. Pipe apron strings in white decorator frosting. Decorate the apron with more frosting.

Pad and pen: Cut out 4 rectangles from the remaining chewy candies, each about $^3/_4$ x $^1/_2$ inch. Impress cuts into one end and secure to the hands with decorator frosting. Shape tiny yellow fondant pens and secure to the pads, adding small clips using red decorator frosting.

Shoes: Pipe dainty black shoes using black decorator frosting.

Hair: Use black decorator frosting to pipe hair onto each head and position more strips of chewy candies above the bangs (fringes).

Face: Pipe small mouths using red decorator frosting and eyes using black decorator frosting.

try me too! page 120

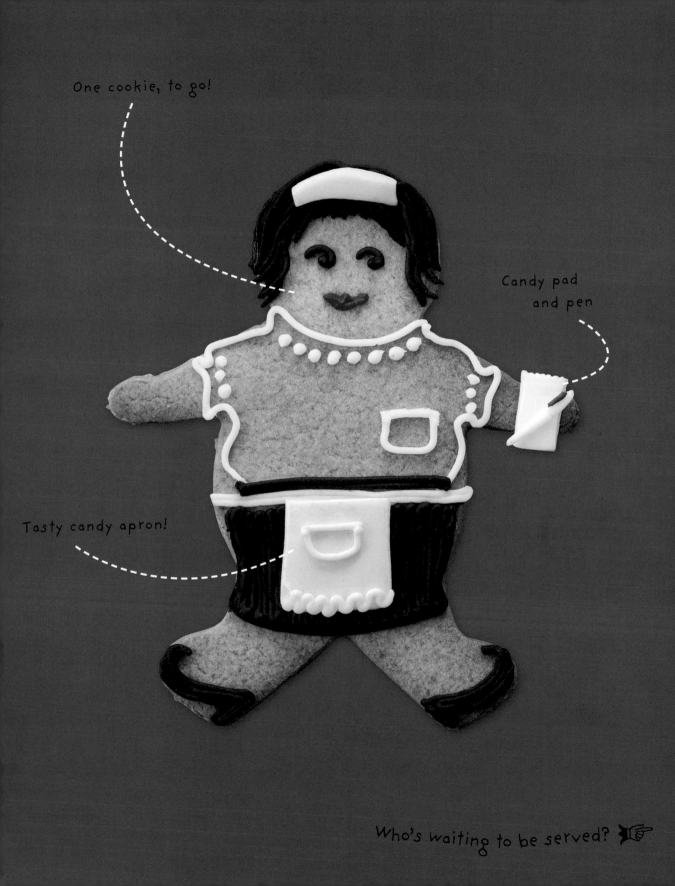

Rock Star

Ingredients

- Glacé icing (see page 8)
- 4 gingerbread cookies
- 3 oz black rolled fondant
- Confectioners' sugar, for dusting
- Small piece of white rolled fondant
- Black icing pen or black food coloring
- Tubes of red, white, and black decorator frosting
- 3 oz red rolled fondant
- Edible silver food coloring
- 1 1/2 oz yellow rolled fondant
- Confectioner's glaze (optional)

Equipment

- Small spatula
- Rolling pin
- Gingerbread cutter
- Craft knife
- Paintbrush
- Toothpicks

Leather pants: Using a spatula, spread a little glacé icing over the lower half of each gingerbread cookie. For each pair of pants, roll out a quarter of the black fondant on a surface dusted with confectioners' sugar until about $1/16$ inch thick. Cut out pants shapes with the cutter, trimming off the fondant at the waist and ankles. Secure in place.

Sneakers: Roll out the white fondant and cut out white sneakers. Secure in place with glacé icing. Paint markings with a black icing pen or food coloring and pipe laces with red decorator frosting.

Vest and jacket: Use white decorator frosting to pipe diagonal lines about $1/8$ inch apart over the top half of each gingerbread body, first in one direction then the other, to resemble a vest. Pipe a straight line across the top and bottom edges.

For each jacket, thinly roll out a quarter of the red fondant until about $1/16$ inch thick. Cut out a jacket shape with the cutter. Trim off the fondant at the neck, wrists, and waist. Cut a $3/4$-inch-wide strip out of the front of each jacket so that the white vest shows through when secured in place.

Pipe dots of white decorator frosting along the edges of the jacket to make a zipper. Once hardened, paint the dots with edible silver food coloring.

Hair: Pipe plenty of hair using black decorator frosting.

Face: Pipe a line of black decorator frosting across the top of each face, then secure 2 semicircles of black fondant below the line for sunglasses. Pipe small noses and mouths in red decorator frosting. Use the black icing pen or food coloring to dot the chin with "stubble."

Guitar: For each guitar, mold a little yellow fondant into a curvy guitar shape, about $1\frac{3}{4}$ inches long. Roll out a thin strip of white fondant, about $2\frac{1}{2}$ x $\frac{1}{4}$ inches and slightly thicker at one end, to make the neck of the guitar. Slide a toothpick into one end of the guitar to support the white fondant. Rest the fondant on top and use a dampened paintbrush to secure it in place where it overlaps the yellow fondant. Use red and black decorator frosting to pipe the guitar details. Secure in place with decorator frosting.

Finishing touch: If desired, use a paintbrush to brush the black fondant pants with confectioner's glaze, giving a shiny finish.

Disco Girl

Ingredients

- Blue and red food coloring
- Vanilla buttercream (see page 8)
- 4 gingerbread cookies
- 2$\frac{1}{2}$ oz dark blue rolled fondant
- Confectioners' sugar, for dusting
- Tubes of white and black decorator frosting
- 1$\frac{1}{2}$ oz ivory rolled fondant
- 2 oz light brown rolled fondant
- Pink and pearl or silver dragees
- $\frac{1}{2}$ oz black rolled fondant
- Edible silver food coloring

Equipment

- Paper pastry bag (see page 13)
- Rolling pin
- Gingerbread cutter
- Craft knife
- Paintbrush

T-shirt: Beat blue food coloring into the buttercream, adding a little at a time until the desired shade is reached. Put in a paper pastry bag and snip off the merest tip. Use to pipe the outline of a skimpy T-shirt onto each gingerbread cookie. Fill in the shape with more piping, working vertical lines across the T-shirt.

Jeans: Pipe a little more buttercream over the lower half of each cookie, leaving the feet uncovered. For each pair of jeans, roll out a quarter of the blue fondant on a surface lightly dusted with confectioners' sugar until about $\frac{1}{16}$ inch thick. Cut out low-cut jeans with the gingerbread cutter, trimming off the fondant below the waist and at the ankles. Secure in place. Use white decorator frosting to pipe stitches around the edges and to shape a pocket.

Boots: Pipe a little buttercream over the feet of each cookie. For each pair of boots, thinly roll out a quarter of the ivory fondant. Press each leg of the gingerbread cutter into the fondant, trimming off the top edge in a straight line. Cut out deep notches for high heels and secure in place. Pipe a line of black decorator frosting along the lower edges of the boots.

Hair: Trace and cut out the Disco Girl's hair template (see opposite). Roll out the light brown fondant until about $\frac{1}{16}$ inch thick and cut around the template. Repeat to give 4 sets of hair. Mark shallow cuts with the tip of a craft knife and secure in place with buttercream.

Face: Using red and blue food coloring and a fine paintbrush paint an eye and half a mouth on each cookie, so the face shows only slightly through the hair.

Finishing touches: Pipe plenty of bangles over the arms using black and white decorator frosting. Pipe a long "necklace" using white decorator frosting and press pink and pearl or silver dragees into it and into one of the bracelets. Shape 4 small microphones, each about $3/4$ inch long, in black fondant with a slightly rounded end. Paint the rounded ends silver with edible silver food coloring. Secure to the hands with decorator frosting.

Magician

Ingredients

- Vanilla buttercream (see page 8)
- 4 gingerbread cookies
- 2 oz white rolled fondant
- Confectioners' sugar, for dusting
- Tube of black decorator frosting
- 5 oz black rolled fondant
- 2 oz purple rolled fondant
- Small piece of red rolled fondant
- 1 strawberry-flavor licorice

Equipment

- Small spatula
- Rolling pin
- Craft knife
- Gingerbread cutter
- Paintbrush

Shirt: Using a spatula, spread a little buttercream over the body area of each gingerbread cookie, leaving the hands and feet uncovered. Roll out the white fondant on a surface dusted with confectioners' sugar until about $1/16$ inch thick. Cut out four 2-inch squares and secure to the cookies so the tops of the squares are level with the necks. (Trim off the edges of the fondant if it comes over the sides of the cookies.)

Cut 8 small triangles of white fondant from the trimmings and secure for collars. Pipe a row of buttons down each shirt front with black decorator frosting.

Suit: For each pair of pants, roll out a little black fondant until about $1/16$ inch thick. Cut out pants shapes with the gingerbread cutter, trimming off the fondant just below the waist and at the ankles. Secure in place. (The black trouser fondant should meet the white shirt fondant. If it overlaps, cut a little off the trouser fondant.)

For each jacket, roll out a quarter of the remaining black fondant. Cut out a jacket shape with the gingerbread cutter, trimming off the fondant at the neck, wrists, and waist. Cut a deep "v" out of the front of each jacket. Position over the shirts, securing with a dampened paintbrush.

Cloak: For each cloak, roll out the purple fondant and cut out 2 curved pieces, each about 1 x $1/2$ inch, and secure around the neck for the top of the cloak. Cut out 2 rectangles, each about 2 x $1/2$ inches, and secure to the sides of the cookie with a little buttercream.

Shoes: Mold shoes out of red fondant and position with a little buttercream, adding laces with piped black decorator frosting.

Face and hair: Pipe eyes using black decorator frosting, finishing with eyebrows, one raised. Add mouths using small pieces of strawberry-flavor licorice, securing with black frosting. Pipe black hair.

Finishing touches: Shape bow ties using the red fondant trimmings and secure at the join of the collar pieces. Roll a long thin piece of black fondant under your fingertips and cut into four $1\frac{3}{4}$-inch lengths. Secure pieces of red fondant to one end with a dampened paintbrush. Allow to harden on parchment paper before securing to hands with a dot of decorator frosting.

Ghost

Ingredients

- Glacé icing (see page 8)
- 4 gingerbread cookies
- 2¹/₂ oz blue rolled fondant
- Confectioners' sugar, for dusting
- 1 oz yellow rolled fondant
- 8 small blue candy drops
- Tube of white decorator frosting
- 6 oz white rolled fondant
- ¹/₂ oz black rolled fondant

Equipment

- Small spatula
- Rolling pin
- Gingerbread cutter
- Craft knife
- Paintbrush

Pants: Using a spatula, spread a thin layer of glacé icing over the lower half of each gingerbread cookie, leaving the feet uncovered. For each pair of pants, roll out a quarter of the blue fondant on a surface lightly dusted with confectioners' sugar until about ¹/₁₆ inch thick. Cut out pants shapes with the gingerbread cutter, trimming off the fondant at the waist and ankles. Secure in place.

Slippers: Mold small pieces of the yellow fondant into slippers to match the foot shape and secure in place with a little glacé icing. For the pompoms, secure a candy drop to the top of each slipper using a dot of white decorator frosting.

Ghostly sheet: Using a spatula, spread a little glacé icing over the top half of each body and head. For each sheet, roll out a quarter of the white fondant until about ¹/₁₆ inch thick. Rest the gingerbread cutter gently over the surface of the fondant and use it as a guide to cutting out a sheet shape. Cut around the head and along the tops of the arms, tapering the fondant down to the widest part of the body. Lift the cutter away, then, using a craft knife, cut away the lower edge to create a jagged effect, as in the picture. Secure in place.

Pipe a line of white decorator frosting along the jagged edge. Roll small balls of black fondant and position for eyes, securing with a dampened paintbrush.

Robber

Ingredients

- Vanilla buttercream (see page 8)
- 4 gingerbread cookies
- 1 licorice wheel
- 4 thin white chewy candies in any flavor
- Black food coloring
- Small red candies
- Tube of red decorator frosting
- 4 soft strawberry-flavor licorices

Equipment

- Small spatula
- Craft knife
- Scissors
- Paper pastry bag (see page 13)

Striped pullover: Using a spatula, spread a little buttercream over the top half of each gingerbread cookie, leaving the hands and heads uncovered. Unroll the licorice wheel and cut into lengths about the width of the cookie. Press the lengths slightly apart across the buttercream, trimming to fit.

Bobble hat: Using scissors, cut out semicircular shapes from the thin white chewy candies. Make indentations along the lower edge of each semicircle with a craft knife and secure in place with buttercream. Beat black food coloring into the remaining buttercream, adding a little at a time until the desired shade is reached. Put in a paper pastry bag and snip off the merest tip. Pipe a bobble at the top of the hat and a band near to the bottom edge.

Face: Use the black buttercream to pipe a mask over each face. Position a piece of red candy for each mouth, securing with red decorator frosting.

Swag bag: Use a craft knife to cut out a notch from each side of one end of each strawberry-flavor licorice. Secure to the arms and decorate with piped black buttercream.

Finishing touches: Use red decorator frosting and black buttercream to pipe the outlines and details of pants, and at the wrists and necklines, as in the picture. Position 2 further strips of black licorice for the shoes, securing in place with black buttercream.

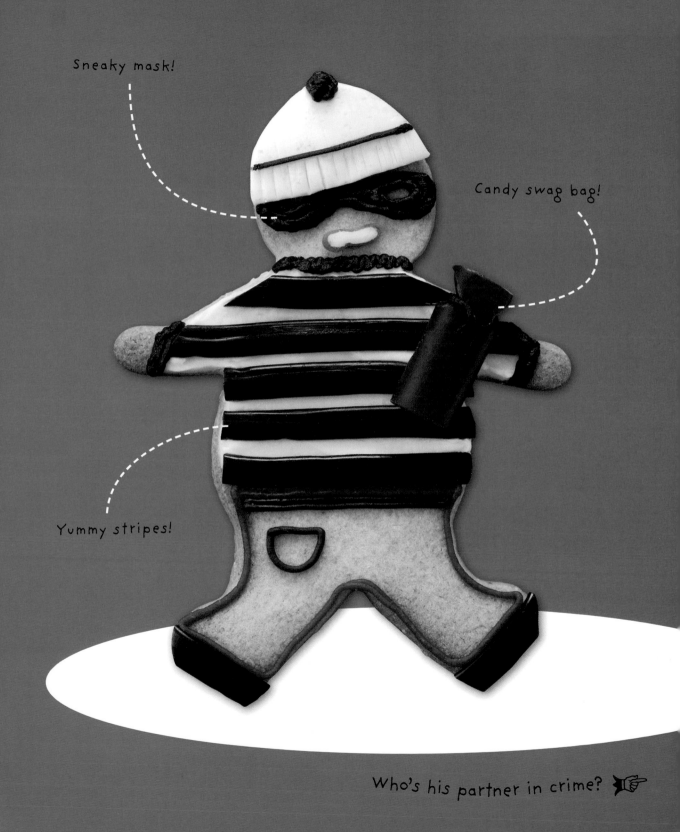

Sneaky mask!

Candy swag bag!

Yummy stripes!

Who's his partner in crime?

Cat Burglar

Ingredients

- Black food coloring
- Vanilla buttercream (see page 8)
- 4 gingerbread cookies
- 1 licorice wheel
- Tubes of white and red decorator frosting
- 4 small pink chewy candies
- Silver dragees

Equipment

- Small spatula
- Craft knife
- Paper pastry bag (see page 13)

try me too! page 58

Cat suit: Beat black food coloring into the buttercream, adding a little at a time until the desired shade is reached. Using a spatula, spread a thin layer over the body area of each gingerbread cookie, leaving the hands, feet, and heads uncovered. Unroll the licorice wheel and cut four 2-inch lengths. Position down the fronts of the cookies so the top ends of the licorice are level with the necks.

Pipe lines of white decorator frosting at the wrists and neck of each suit. Pipe a line of white frosting down the center of each licorice strip and finish with a piped zipper at the neck.

Hood: Spread a little more buttercream around the top and sides of each head. Cut out 8 triangular pieces from the licorice and secure in place for cat's ears.

Face: Put the remaining black buttercream in a paper pastry bag and snip off the merest tip. Use to pipe a mask over the eye area of each gingerbread face. Pipe a raised edge around the inside curve of each hood. Pipe small red mouths in red decorator frosting.

Backpack: Using scissors, cut the chewy candies so they can be fitted to one side of each body. Secure in place with black buttercream, then add a piped strap of red decorator frosting. Pipe a red outline around each pack.

Finishing touches: Pipe outlines of heeled boots in black buttercream and press rows of silver dragees into the black buttercream of each body to represent stolen jewels bursting out of the backpack.

Bride

Ingredients

- Glacé icing (see page 8)
- 4 gingerbread cookies
- 5 oz white rolled fondant
- Confectioners' sugar, for dusting
- Tube of white decorator frosting
- 2 oz yellow rolled fondant
- 1 tablespoon chocolate hazelnut spread
- 2 oz pale pink rolled fondant
- 2 oz lilac rolled fondant
- 1 candied cherry

Equipment

- Parchment paper, for tracing
- Pencil
- Scissors
- Rolling pin
- Craft knife
- Small spatula
- Toothpick
- Paper pastry bag (see page 13)
- Small cake decorator's flower cutters or ready-made sugar flowers

Dress: Trace and cut out the Bride's dress template (see page 127). Roll out the white fondant on a surface dusted with confectioners' sugar until about $1/16$ inch thick. Cut around the dress template and repeat to give 4 dresses. Using a spatula, spread a little glacé icing over the body area of each gingerbread cookie, and secure each dress in place.

Make folds along the lower edges of the skirts by lifting the fondant at intervals with a toothpick and pinching the fondant around the toothpick so the folds are held in place. Use white decorator frosting to pipe a curved waistband around each dress.

Hair and veil: Trace and cut out the Bride's hair template (see opposite) and veil template (see page 127). Roll out the white fondant trimmings and cut around the veil template. Repeat to give 4 veils. Spread a little glacé icing over the center of each veil and gently press a gingerbread head down onto it.

Roll out the yellow fondant until about $1/16$ inch thick and cut around the hair template. Repeat to give 4 sets of hair. Secure in place with a little glacé icing. Use the white fondant trimmings to shape little veil tops and secure in place. Put the chocolate hazelnut spread in a paper pastry bag and snip off the merest tip. Use to decorate the hair, as in the picture.

Pearls: Pipe a thin line of pearls around the neck and wrists of each cookie using white decorator frosting.

Slippers: Cut out slender slipper shapes in pink fondant and secure with glacé icing.

Flowers: Spread glacé icing over one wrist and one side of each dress. Thinly roll out the pink and lilac fondant and cut out tiny flowers using the cutters. Press them into the glacé icing as you go. (Alternatively, use ready-made sugar flowers.) Add a flower to each slipper and some to the top of the hair. Pipe a dot of white decorator frosting into the center of each.

Face: Use the chocolate spread to pipe eyes. Add small balls of white fondant for noses and little pieces of candied cherry for the mouths, securing with white decorator frosting.

Groom

Ingredients

- 3 tablespoons chocolate hazelnut spread
- 4 gingerbread cookies
- 3 oz black rolled fondant
- Confectioners' sugar, for dusting
- Tube of white decorator frosting
- Small piece of pink rolled fondant
- Small piece of lilac rolled fondant
- 1 candied cherry
- 1 oz gray rolled fondant

Equipment

- Parchment paper, for tracing
- Pencil
- Scissors
- Rolling pin
- Craft knifte
- Small spatula
- Paper pastry bag (see page 13)
- Small cake decorator's flower cutter or ready-made sugar flowers

Jacket: Trace and cut out the Groom's jacket template (see page 126). Roll out the black fondant on a surface dusted with confectioners' sugar until about $^1/_{16}$ inch thick and cut around the template. Repeat to give 4 jackets. Using a spatula, spread a little chocolate hazelnut spread over the jacket area of each gingerbread cookie and secure the jackets in place. Put the remaining chocolate spread in a paper pastry bag and snip off the merest tip. Use to pipe cuffs and a tiny button on each jacket.

Pants and shoes: Pipe vertical "pin stripes" from the waist down to the feet using the chocolate spread. Roll out the black fondant trimmings and cut out shoes. Secure in place with chocolate spread.

Cravat: Pipe white decorator frosting into the neck area of each cookie for a shirt. Cut 4 teardrop shapes out of pink fondant and secure for a cravat. Pipe diagonal lines of chocolate spread over the pink fondant.

Buttonhole: Thinly roll out the lilac fondant and cut out 4 flowers using the cutter. Secure onto each jacket with white decorator frosting. (Alternatively, use ready-made sugar flowers.) Pipe a dot of white decorator frosting into the center of each.

Hair and face: Use the chocolate spread to pipe curly hair and eyes. Add small balls of white fondant for noses and little pieces of candied cherry for the mouths, securing with white decorator frosting.

Top hat: Trace and cut out the Groom's top hat template (see below). Roll out the gray fondant until about $\frac{1}{16}$ inch thick and cut around the template. Repeat to give 4 hats. Use black fondant trimmings to shape ribbons to fix around the top hats. Secure to the hands with decorator frosting.

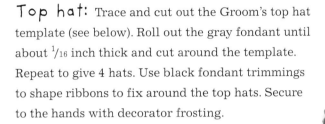

Templates

52 / Mermaid's tail

124 / Groom's jacket

44 / Angel's wings

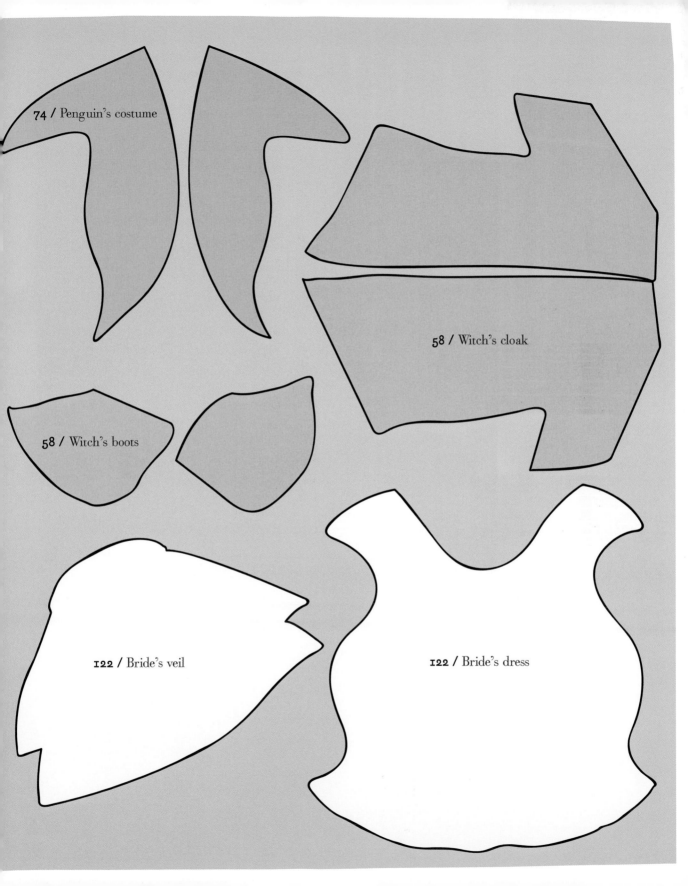

74 / Penguin's costume

58 / Witch's cloak

58 / Witch's boots

122 / Bride's veil

122 / Bride's dress

Source List

Internet sources for decorating ingredients and sugarcraft equipment supplies. Many of the companies also have retail locations.

USA

A.C. Moore
Online and retail supplier
Tel. 1-800-ACMOORE
www.acmoore.com

Global Sugar Art
Online supplier
Tel. 1-800-420-6088
www.globalsugarart.com

Jo-Ann Fabric and Craft Store
Online and retail supplier
Tel. 1-888-739-4120
www.joann.com

Michaels Stores, Inc.
Online and retail supplier
Tel. 1-800-MICHAELS
www.michaels.com

N.Y. Cake & Baking Dist.
Online supplier
56 West 22nd Street
NY, NY 10021
Tel. 212-675-CAKE
www.nycake.com

Pfeil & Holing
Online supplier
Tel. 1-800-247-7955
www.cakedeco.com

Wilton Homewares Store
Online and retail supplier
Tel. 1-800-794-5866
www.wilton.com

Canada

Creative Cutters
Online supplier
1-888-805-3444
www.creativecutters.com

Golda's Kitchen
Online supplier
Tel. 1-866-465-3299
www.goldaskitchen.com

Michaels Stores, Inc.
Online and retail supplier
Tel. 1-800-MICHAELS
www.michaels.com

UK

Almond Art
Online supplier
Unit 15/16, Faraday Close
Gorse Lane Industrial Estate
Clacton-on-Sea
Essex CO15 4TR
Tel. 01255 223 322
www.almondart.com

Blue Ribbon Sugarcraft Centre
Online and retail supplier
29 Walton Road
East Molesey
Surrey KT8 0DH
Tel. 020 8941 1591
www.blueribbons.co.uk

Jane Asher Party Cakes
Online and retail supplier
24 Cale Street
London SW3 3QU
Tel. 020 7584 6177
www.jane-asher.co.uk

Squires Shop and School
Online and retail supplier
Squires House
3 Waverley Lane
Farnham
Surrey GU9 8BB
Tel. 0845 22 55 671
www.squires-group.co.uk

Australia & New Zealand

Cake Deco
Online and retail supplier
Shop 7, Port Philip Arcade
232 Flinders Street
Melbourne, Victoria
Australia
Tel. 03 9654 5335
www.cakedeco.com.au

Milly's
Online and retail supplier
273 Ponsonby Road
Auckland
New Zealand
Tel. 0800 200 123
www.millyskitchen.co.nz

South Africa

Kadies Bakery Supplies
Online and retail supplier
Kingfisher Shopping Centre
Kingfisher Drive
Fourways
Gauteng
South Africa
Tel. 027 11 465-5572
www.kadies.co.za